Games, Powers & Democracies

Gianluca Sgueo
Foreword by Stefaan Verhulst

BUP

Copyright © 2018 Bocconi University Press
EGEA S.p.A.

EGEA S.p.A.
Via Salasco, 5 - 20136 Milan, Italy
Phone + 39 02 5836.5751 - Fax +39 02 5836.5753
egea.edizioni@unibocconi.it - www.egeaeditore.it

All rights reserved, including but not limited to translation, total or partial adaptation, reproduction, and communication to the public by any means on any media (including microfilms, films, photocopies, electronic or digital media), as well as electronic information storage and retrieval systems. For more information or permission to use material from this text, see the website www.egeaeditore.it
Given the characteristics of Internet, the publisher is not responsible for any changes of address and contents of the websites mentioned.

First Edition: May 2018

ISBN Domestic Edition 978-88-99902-26-1
ISBN International Edition 978-88-85486-46-1
ISBN Epub Edition 978-88-85486-57-7
ISBN Mobipoket Edition 978-88-85486-58-4

Table of Contents

Acknowledgment   XI

Foreword: Towards a Science of Gamification and Its Relationship to Governance and Democracy   XIII

1. What if Government Was a Game?   1
1. Not your average tetris   2
2. Imagining the future of public power   4
3. Gamification, governance and regulators   5
4. Innovation and tradition   7
5. Technologies and public power   9
6. Increased convergence, higher expectations   13
7. Escaping anachronism   15
8. Conceptual shifts   17
9. Gamification at crossroads no. 1 - nudging   19
10. Gamification at crossroads no. 2 - democratic Innovations   21
11. Gamification at crossroads no. 3 - crowdsourcing   22
12. Gamification at crossroads no. 4 - civic tech   25
13. The era of disbelief   28
14. Regulators in crisis   31
15. The odd paradox   33
16. The participatory makeover   37
17. Fiscal austerity, the costs of (non-)innovating   39

18. Regulatory complexity, obliged to innovate	41
19. The open questions of gamified governance	43
20. The structure of the volume	47

2. A Cursory Investigation into Gamification — 49
1. Gamification in political communication — 50
2. The politicisation of games — 51
3. Gamification and the business sector — 53
4. Gamified media — 55
5. Games and universities — 57
6. Gamified activism — 58
7. The gamification of climate change activism — 62

3. Games, Rewards and the Exercise of Public Power — 65
1. Mayor for a day — 67
2. Design is key — 70
3. Civic currencies — 72
4. Where is the red balloon? — 73
5. Be kind to your neighbours — 75
6. Participated budgets — 77
7. Taxonomy of national gamified governance — 78
8. Vultures with GoPros — 81
9. Speed camera lotteries and melodic highways — 83
10. Incumbent and critical democracies — 84

4. Gamification Beyond Borders — 89
1. Gamified supranational governance — 92
2. Social innovators and young scientists — 94
3. Storytellers, innovators, connectors and includers — 95
4. Taxonomy of supranational gamified governance — 95
5. Pop hunters, maps and ozone molecules — 98
6. World wonders and inflation rates — 100

Table of Contents   VII

7. Mobile phones and grains of rice   102
8. The 'Evokation'   103
9. Regulatory experimentalism   104
10. Blocks and youth workers   106

5. Gamified Publics   109
1. Hard-core participants vs. unqualified masses   110
2. Breaking free from quantitative assessments   113
3. Constituting the demos   115
4. Ties and engagements   117
5. Gamified publics no. 1 - policy-entrepreneurs   119
6. Gamified publics No. 2 - citizen-lobbyists   122
7. Capturing the regulators   124
8. Gamified publics no. 3 - citizen-activists   126
9. Gamified publics and governance no. 1 - prosumerism   129
10. Gamified publics and governance no. 2 - collective intelligence   130
11. Gamified publics and governance no. 3 - network theory   133

6. The Dark Side of Gamified Governance   135
1. Dangers of incentives   136
2. The hollowing of the state   138
3. Digitally divided   140
4. Digitally excluded   142
5. Digitally ignorant   143
6. Linguistic barriers   145
7. Policy cycle: front and back ends   146
8. Policy areas   148
9. The new feudal society   149

Conclusions: The Only Winning Move Is (Not) to Play 153
1. The puzzle of effectiveness 154
2. Making smart uses of collective intelligence 156
3. Ethics as usual 158
4. Privacy matters 158
5. Embracing failure 160

Writing is an inherently painful process. It takes time, demands concentration and focus. When writing, you close doors to keep out the rest of the world and its distractions. Some are doors you would never close under different circumstances.
This book is dedicated to Claudia, my wife, who keeps me happy when workloads converge, and to Elettra, my daughter, who never stops making me smile and think. Thank you both for your patience and love while my head was elsewhere, behind closed doors.

Acknowledgements

This book is a part of a broader research project focused on the various uses of gamification within a number of sectors (from public governance to non-profit advocacy). Most of the data and information related to the case studies analysed in the book draws significantly on, or incorporate parts of, my preparatory research for the course on 'Gamification in Politics, Business & Communications: An Interdisciplinary Approach' that I teach at Vesalius College, Vrije University in Brussels. Other parts of the book have benefited from contributions made by Alessandro El Khoury, Francesco Berti and Marco Meloni during the panel on 'Gamification Strategies for Non-Profit Advocacy' which I chaired at the International Conference on Democracy and Participation in the 21st Century, held at the Lisbon School of Economics and Management, University of Lisbon, in July 2017. I am also grateful for comments on an early 'gamification and participatory democracy' paper I presented at the University of Vienna's conference on 'Activation—Self-Management—Overload' in September 2017.

Several colleagues provided direct comments on early drafts of this book, in whole or in part, improving it immeasurably. Special thanks go to Professor Sabino Cassese, who helped me strengthen the theoretical background of this research. I am also grateful to Maria Luisa Torchia, Giulio Napolitano and Edoardo Chiti, all of whom provided useful comments on an earlier version of this book during a lunch seminar at the Istituto di Ricerche sulla Pubblica Amministrazione, Rome, in 2016.

I am particularly thankful to Professor Alberto Alemanno (HEC Paris), who read and commented at various stages during the drafting process, and Giovanni Allegretti (Centre for Social Studies, University of Coimbra), who involved me in the amazing experience of Empaville, a role-playing game on participatory budgeting. I would never have dreamed of writing a book on gamification without their help, inspiration and guidance. I want to extend my thanks to Stefaan Verhulst of the New York University (NYU) GovLab. His weekly Digest is an incredible source of inspiration and an intellectual stimulus.

I would like to express my gratitude to students in my 'global advocacy' class at Vesalius College for challenging my assumptions during the course with their compelling questions and insights. I have benefited greatly from the opportunity to present lectures at the college based on parts of this research while the work was still in progress. Special thanks go to Tavishi Rai, a passionate student who volunteered to help me with mining data and searching for materials.

The ideas exposed in this book have also been shaped by discussions with many students at NYU Florence, particularly via the public talks that I have organised since 2016. For this reason, I wish to express my warmest thanks to Ellyn Toscano, director of the NYU Florentine campus, Megan Metters, coordinator of 'La Pietra Dialogues', and the wonderful people working with them.

I am also grateful to Sarah Tighe, who did a great job in editing the manuscript, providing enormously valuable and extensive feedback on both the content and the form. I am solely responsible for any errors that appear in the book.

Finally, I would like to express my profound appreciation to my publisher Egea for believing in this project and being my guide and mentor in the process that transformed the original draft into the final version of the book.

Foreword: Towards a Science of Gamification and its Relationship to Governance and Democracy

by Stefaan Verhulst[1]

Every century poses its own challenges, but those of the twenty-first are already shaping up to be uniquely complex and intractable. From climate change to economic inequality to terrorism and migration, countries around the world face problems that have no easy solutions. Compounding the difficulty is a crisis in governance. This crisis is one of both effectiveness and legitimacy. The two issues are mutually reinforcing; as a result, our problems grow worse, and solutions seem ever further out of reach.

It is increasingly clear that we not only need new ideas but also new methods for arriving at, implementing and experimenting with new approaches.

This book explores one possible method that can help mitigate some of today's governance problems: gamification.

Gamification, as Gianluca Sgueo shows in the following chapters, is not, in fact, a completely new approach to governance. Its use (in a widely varying form) can be traced at least as far back as Plato. But the use of gamified elements for problem-solving—

---

[1] Chief Research and Development Officer of the Governance Laboratory @NYU (GovLab).

beyond the traditional connotation of games as entertainment—has reached new prominence in recent years with the rise of digital platforms, and especially the near-universal adoption of social media.

Gamification is certainly not a panacea for all our societal ills, and it poses various challenges of its own (notably those linked to privacy, design and inclusion). But, combined with other innovations and methods—such as behavioural economics and collective intelligence—it offers a valuable, fascinating and under-explored approach to governance in the twenty-first century.

The governance potential offered by gamification stems primarily from the avenues it offers for greater (motivation towards) participation, inclusion and, consequently, transparency across the full policy life cycle—from agenda setting to solution ideation, policy development, implementation, enforcement and review of effectiveness. For instance:

- Agenda setting: By incentivising and encouraging citizen interaction on various platforms and portals, gamification can help public and civic actors indicate preferences or experiences to set the agenda and define problems and priorities.
- Ideation and design of solutions: Greater user interaction also allows policy-makers to draw on a wider and more dispersed range of expertise, thus helping identify and co-create new approaches to so-called 'wicked problems'.
- Enforcement and feedback: In addition, gamification can play a role in ensuring accountability: citizens have a valuable part to play in enforcement and implementation of government schemes, and gamified methods can help manifest this potential by, for example, incentivising citizens to rate or otherwise provide feedback on government schemes.

By encouraging greater citizen participation in the processes and institutions of governance, and in the process strengthening the effectiveness of governance, gamification can help address the previously mentioned legitimacy and effectiveness deficit facing democracies around the world.

It is important to note, however, that gamification on its own is an incomplete solution, and might be most effective as a complementary tool to other approaches that are directed at increasing citizen participation and interaction. Such tools can include nudging or crowdsourcing mechanisms that are more generally directed at gathering citizen feedback (with or without gaming aspects).

In addition, the effectiveness of gamification can be enhanced through greater use of rapid experimentation and feedback loops, both of which provide opportunities for quick iteration and policy refinement; the use of these feedback loops (and, more generally, an agile approach to gamification) are an essential component of the innovation toolkit that can and should be deployed by policy-makers alongside gamification.

The complementary and holistic use of these various approaches is critical in order to address one of the perceived shortcomings of gamification, namely its limited approach to representativeness. As with any strategy designed to elicit greater citizen responsiveness, the effectiveness of gamification will depend to a significant degree on how wide a net it casts in reaching citizens. Tools or platforms that gather feedback from only a narrow range of society will inevitably also impact the perceived legitimacy of governance outcomes. For this reason, it is essential that a gamification approach is also accompanied by strategies to ensure participation by the widest possible selection of stakeholders and interest groups. Such strategies can include outreach efforts, including education and awareness building; and a design approach that is focused on inclusiveness, for example by taking into account different technical capacities and languages in a given country or society.

All these topics—and many more—are covered in far greater detail in the subsequent chapters. Overall, this book provides a comprehensive overview of a generally under-examined policy innovation that nonetheless holds significant promise. It helps consider how—and, indeed, if—society can benefit from motivations and actions that may also be fun—not usually associated with the often dry topics of governance and policy-making. It also expands the existing literature of gamification, beyond how to use game features for health and wellness, education and customer satisfaction, to include governing.

Ultimately, this book is a call for a much deeper examination of how we innovate and improve the way we solve public problems, and for a dedicated science of gamification and its relationship to governance and democracy.

1. What if Government Was a Game?

Black Mirror is an award-winning British TV anthology that explores real and imagined fears and paranoia around technology. In 'Nosedive', the opening episode of the third season, we are introduced to Lacie, a woman desperate to boost her social media score. In a world where people rate each personal interaction on a one-to-five stars scale, an individual's average rating has significant influence on societal status. When the episode begins, Lacie is rated 4.2, which is a good, solid score but below what might be considered 'elite'. But Lacie is ambitious - she wants to raise her score to 4.5 and qualify for a luxury apartment. After her initial attempts to impress people fail, she hires a consultant who suggests she gets approval from highly ranked people whose ratings carry more weight. When she is subsequently invited to the high-society wedding of a childhood friend, she believes her own score will increase once she gives a fantastic speech to wedding guests (all of whom are rated 4.5 or higher). But her efforts have disastrous consequences. A number of incidents shatter her rating, destroying her freedom to book a flight, rent a car, and eventually, attend the wedding. By the episode's conclusion, Lacie is removed from society -imprisoned, with the rating technology stripped from her body. The episode closes with Lacie getting into a heated argument with another prisoner, realising how liberating it is to express herself without worrying about being rated.

There is a lot in 'Nosedive' that is reminiscent of a video game. A positive rating is accompanied with a high-spirited warble, whereas a negative score is accented with a gloomy tune. Life is a constant struggle for higher scores. Scaling up means cooler friends, healthier food, superior services—in summary: a better life. But it is no easy feat; getting high ratings requires full-time dedication and strategy. It is extremely time consuming, and not without risks. It seems like, for want of a better phrase, hard work.

It would be easy to dismiss the world in 'Nosedive' as science fiction, a parallel universe existing only on the screens of televisions and smart devices. Except for one factor. Much of what is narrated in the episode seems to be already happening in reality. So, what if the world depicted in 'Nosedive' was much closer to our own than we realise? What if the pursuit for better ratings, or their equivalent, was already part of our lives? What if governments, public bodies and organisations were already using technology in similar ways to those in 'Nosedive', transforming the exercise of public power into a game?

1. Not your average tetris

Picture a government that measures civic value on a numbered scale, with civic performances tallied on leader boards, like a football match. Imagine if civic value was viewed as a game played by everyday citizens, sometimes in competition, other times working in harmony towards a common goal. And imagine that winners were celebrated (and losers blamed) collectively—in a sort of Gibsonian 'consensual hallucination'.[1] Sound a little far-fetched? Think again. Residents of Santa Monica, in California, can now swipe left or right on a Tinder-like website, to like or dislike the municipal council's proposed changes to their local neighbourhoods. Citizens of Boston share information on traffic, criminality,

---

[1] See W. GIBSON, *Neuromancer*, Ace Books, 1984.

1. What if Government Was a Game?

Wi-Fi availability and waste management with the office of the mayor. In so doing, they help to evaluate the performance of their city, which is rated on a graded scale, and shared on a publicly accessible digital dashboard. In New Mexico, residents of Albuquerque can monitor 'acts of [civic] kindness' with a dedicated app. Thousands of miles south, Peruvians can track vultures trained to seek out illegal garbage dumps via GoPro cameras and GPS devices fitted to their bodies. Across the pond, Europe is no exception. Dubliners receive up to €200 in vouchers by helping the city council monitor public toilets and fountains located in the city parks. Madrid residents with ideas about how to improve community life can share them online via a dedicated website. Ideas with enough interest and 'likes', may be voted on by the municipal council and actually implemented. Similarly, residents of Barcelona can join an online consultation forum, present their ideas on issues regarding local public services, and rate those of others by supporting or opposing them. Heading east, we meet Muscovites who are rewarded with points every time they vote on a dedicated e-voting platform. Points can be redeemed to pay parking tickets and metro fares, or to enter contests to win opera tickets. In the Chinese city of Suining, citizens are rewarded or deducted points according to their social behaviour. Do you take care of a family member? You earn fifty points. Have you been convicted for drunk driving? Fifty points are deducted. Depending on your overall grade, you could be given priority in employment, or even denied access to some social services.

Moving beyond national borders, the story continues. If you resist the temptation to use your mobile phone for fifteen minutes, or correctly guess the meaning of a fancy English word, you can trigger donations sponsored by the United Nations (UN). Are you good at coming up with solutions to tackle global problems like famine, climate change or diversity? There is a game for that, too. All you have to do is to engage in a weekly game called *Evoke*, and liaise with players from all over the world. You might have a chance to have your ideas evaluated (and implemented) by the World Bank's (WB) officials, in Washington.

Gamified public power is much closer to reality than it may first appear - and as Eugeny Morozov ironically points out, it looks nothing like 'your average Tetris'.[2]

2. Imagining the future of public power

So how should this make us feel? Should we be glad? Worried even? Probably both. This is what this book intends to cover. It is an investigation of strategies of 'gamification' by national and supranational regulators. In this respect, the mode of analysis of this book is largely descriptive, in that it offers a comparative overview of several forms of governance that attempt to innovate through entailing game elements. Beyond that, it aims at exploring the potential—but also at understanding the limits—of the use of gamification in the public sector.

It is worth remembering that gamified governance's legal, societal, political and cultural challenges remain unexplored. Almost no empirical testing has been done on the number of legal regimes interested in this phenomenon, and to identify what kind of capabilities public regulators must develop to leverage the benefits of gamification and deliver public outcomes effectively.

To date, no research has attempted to determine if and how gamification strategies differentiate across policy stages and areas. Above all, no study has determined whether gamified governance fosters or discourages civic engagement. And although it probably goes beyond the capacity of this book to resolve all these challenges, it is my modest aim to contribute to the task of imagining what the exercise of public power might become, including its promises and threats.

---

[2] See E. MOROZOV, *To Save Everything, Click Here*, Penguin, 2013.

3. Gamification, governance and regulators

At the outset, all this information might be a little hard to process. So, let's just take a step back for a moment and briefly clarify some of the terminology related to gamification, governance and the regulators described in this book. In its most commonly used and widely accepted definition, gamification describes the introduction of game design elements (badges, points, levels, rankings, challenges, virtual currencies, etc.) into non-game contexts, with the former aimed at making the latter more enjoyable.[3]

A common misconception is that gamification and games are the same thing - they're not. The use of game mechanics, as Alan Chorney puts it, does not necessarily make a product a video game.[4] Gamification is comparable - albeit not entirely equivalent - to three concepts. First is 'games with a purpose' - that is, systems that invite individuals to collaborate in performing tasks that require skills that humans possess better than computers (as, for instance, with the practice known as 'image recognition'). Second is 'serious games' - that is, games aimed at teaching or training individuals to perform particular tasks, possibly with the inclusion of game-like enjoyable features. Third is 'loyalty programmes' - that is, economic incentives adopted in business practices, typically in the case of stamp collection. Each of these concepts differ somewhat from each other, but have in common the notion that games may well be used beyond the boundaries of fun and entertainment.

Undeniably, gamification has become a slogan, used and (increasingly often) abused. At one count, a Google search for the term 'gamification' produces more than 9.5 million results - with more than 52,000 appearing in Google Scholar alone. It is also possible

---

[3] See S. DETERDING, D. DIXON, R. KHALED & L. NACKE, 'From game design elements to gamefulness: defining gamification' in *Proceedings of the 15th International Academic MindTrek Conference: Envisioning Future Media Environments*, ACM Press, 2011; B. BURKE, *Gamify: How Gamification Motivates People to Do Extraordinary Things*, Bibliomotion, 2014.
[4] See A.I. CHORNEY, 'Taking the game out of gamification', *Dalhousie Journal of Interdisciplinary Management*, 8.1, 1-14 (2012).

that the term will eventually become outdated as journalistic interests move on to the next buzzword. At present, however, it remains the best definition to capture certain evolutions of innovative policy-making. Gamification, in fact, presents three advantages. First, it allows us to portray a large number of experiences, promoted by different actors, in distant geographical locations and different times. This conceptual broadness is beneficial to elide issues of variance (and instead focus on the commonalities) among the case studies discussed in this book. Second, the notion of gamification has a sufficiently 'neutral' meaning to avoid misleading - that is, ideologically charged - interpretations. By contrast - and this is a third motive for using the term - it can be argued that 'gamification' is sufficiently provocative to define avenues of experimentation in governance by public powers, both national and supranational.

Moving from one buzzword to another: governance. Differently from gamification, governance has no universal definition and has come to mean different things in different contexts. In the context of this book, the concept of governance will be used in its broadest connotation—to refer to all the structures and processes that allow a public authority to conduct affairs. Phrases like 'policy-making' or 'decision-making', it goes without saying, are used as terminological variances of the same concept.

Those 'responsible' for governing are described in this book with a single word: regulators. This definition encompasses domestic and supranational actors. Domestic, or national, regulators are all public authorities charged with regulatory powers and operating within national boundaries. These include governments, parliaments, regional and municipal administrations, independent authorities and agencies, where there are any. Supranational regulators are all institutions of an executive or supervisory nature, established by or in conformity with a treaty, and responsible for the application of rules which it implements itself or which mandates others to implement.[5] Hence supranational regulators include both organisations that are properly described as international organisations - the UN, for instance - and those that instead are termed supranational, the European Union (EU) being a case in point. Of course, international and supranational have fairly specific, and different, meanings in legal terminology, which makes of the simplification adopted in this book one that, in more formalised contexts, would be treated as an unforgivable mistake. In the context of gamified governance, however, international and supranational organisations are equivalent. Similar are the strategies adopted, equivalent the expected outcomes and equal the risks - in short, supranational gamified governance does not make use of (nor does it distinguish between) the legal status of the regulator involved.

4. Innovation and tradition

We earlier asserted that gamification opens up governance to innovative perspectives. Let's now fine-tune this concept a little. In reality, gamified governance combines innovation with tradition. The gamification of the exercise of public power is a very recent phenomenon, and yet it dates back centuries. The term gamification hadn't even been invented twenty years ago. According to some, it was coined by Nick Pelling in 2002. But its first documented use only dates back to a 2008 blog post by Bret Terrill.

Conceptually, however, the application of game design elements, principles and practices in non-game contexts is as old as government itself. Games were part of the inner public sphere in Greek and Roman societies and have existed in some form or other throughout the history of public power. Plato compared politics to a game whose scope is the efficient allocation of the available resources. In ancient

---

[5] For a discussion on the differences and similarities between international and supranational public authorities, See H.J. Hahn, 'International and supranational public authorities', *Law and Contemporary Problems*, 26, 638-665 (1961).

Rome, it was common to provide poorer citizens with free wheat and circus games as a means of gaining political power. Decried by Juvenal in the fourth book of his *Satires*, *panem et circenses* (bread and circuses) was a way to offer easy sources of gratification, distract people from more serious matters and eventually gain their political support. Almost 300 years before Juvenal, the population of Lydia, a region in western Anatolia, invented the games of dices, knucklebones and balls during an eighteen-year famine, as a distraction from hunger. Herodotus, in *The Histories*, wrote that the Lydians played games every second day to forget the need for food. The day after, they stopped the games to eat.

John Gastil and Laura Black go as far as to claim that deliberative processes are inherently gamified.[6] Both decision-making and games are governed by rules, have goals and may turn on unexpected events. Fair enough. What is certainly novel, however, is the attention paid by national and supranational regulators to the motivational and behavioural effects of game mechanisms, and their 'proceduralisation' in policy-making. The records show a dramatic expansion of gamification within the public sector. When the research and advisory firm Gartner acknowledged it for the first time in 2012, it forecasted that, within two years, more than 70% of the top 2,000 public organisations worldwide would have at least one gamified application in place.[7] Since 2013, the company has included gamification among their top-ranking prospects in the 'Hype Cycle for Digital Government Technology' - a cycle that identifies promising technologies for future social innovations. According to the 2014 Hype Cycle for Emerging Technologies, gamification has surpassed the 'Peak of Inflated Expectations' and is expected to reach the 'Plateau of Productivity' in the next five to ten years. Together with robotics, artificial intelligence, biometrics and data, (serious-)

---

[6] See J. Gastil & L. Black, 'Public deliberation as the organizing principle of political communication research', *Journal of Public Deliberation*, 4.1, 1-47 (2007).
[7] See B. Burke, *Gamification 2020: What Is the Future of Gamification?*, Gartner, 2012.

games are recognised among the technological paradigms that are shaping the evolution of public administrations.

5. Technologies and public power

So, gamified behavioural approaches are becoming trendy in national and supranational governance - but why? What causes are contributing to the shift in policy-making from traditional top-down, expert-driven, methods of governance to more experimental approaches? Obviously, several explanations may account for the growing interest in gamification within the public sphere. In this chapter, we describe four: the first, and main, consists of the diffusion of technologies in the public sector; the second relates to the lack of trust in politics and policy-making, and the consequent attempts by regulatory authorities to attract the disillusioned citizenry into public life; the third and fourth consist of financial constraints and regulatory complexity, respectively.

But if one cause of the growing relevance of experimental approaches to governance had to be singled out, it would be the profound impact that new technologies have had on the exercise of public power. With very few exceptions - Hannah Arendt, for example, who expressed her scepticism of the prospects for politics in relation to technology—there has been widespread agreement that, following the advent of information and communication technologies (ICT), the relationship and connections between citizens and public regulators have changed dramatically.

Just consider how technologies have altered how citizens and interest groups locate and access information, communicate and learn from each other, and interact with public powers. And it took less than a century. The first modern computers were used in the 1930s to crack cipher codes of foreign governments. By the 1940s computers were used in the defence establishments of many countries.

In the 1950s and 1960s, public administrations began to use computers to assist in large-scale operations, censuses for instance. But the crucial shift happened in the 1990s, after the global boom of ICT technologies. This is known, in jargon, as the shift from Web 1.0 to Web 2.0 - a term coined in 1999 to describe the new websites: easy to use and interoperable with other systems. Since then the average speed of computation has doubled every eighteen months, with costs of production halving on the same cycle.

The 1990s gave birth to the notion of e-government, used to describe the adoption of ICT technologies as a driver to increase the efficiency and effectiveness of governments. Exactly eighteen years ago, Lawrence Lessig argued futuristically in the pages of the *Harvard Magazine* that 'Code is law', that is to say software, along with laws, social norms and markets, can regulate individual and social behaviour.[8]

Since then, empirical research to measure e-governance has literally exploded. Universities, think tanks and international organisations have created indices to assess different aspects of e-governance. The United Nations Public Administration Network, for instance, publishes an e-government readiness index (E-Government Survey) and an E-Participation Index. The Economist Intelligent Unit curates the E-Readiness Index to measure the use of ICT to strengthen economic and social welfare; the World Economic Forum has created a Networked Readiness Index, while the World Justice Project publishes an Open Government Index.[9]

Thanks to the spread of electronic devices, social interaction costs have lowered radically, and audience numbers have become potentially unlimited. A communication technology such as the internet

---

[8] See L. LESSIG, 'Code is law: on liberty in cyberspace', *Harvard Magazine*, 1 January 2000.
[9] For a comparison of e-government indices, see P.A. TUANO, E.C. LALLANA, L. GARCIA & A. ALEGRE, *Evolving an Open E-Governance Index for Network Societies*, Institute of Development Studies, 2017.

- explained Manuel Castells in 1996[10] - allows anyone to communicate information from any location simultaneously and has scaled up the social pressure to participate in social networks.[11]

Geoff Mulgan took Castell's argument one step further when he argued that the growing connectedness of the world was among the most important social facts of our times.[12] Constant connectedness, argued Mulgan, would force governments to rethink their policies and organisational forms. He was right. Connectedness has become so important that it is measured. The Connectedness Index, published yearly by the consulting firm McKinsey, measures global flows of data, services and people, ranking countries in terms of how connected they are to other countries.[13]

Fast forward to today. There are over three billion people connected online, and more than five billion - predicted to triple by 2020 - connected machines. According to the WB, there are ninety-eight mobile cellular subscriptions per 100 people in the world - a 50% increase since 2007.[14] The daily average of physical interactions each of us has with mobile phones exceeds 2,600.[15] The amount of digital information has surpassed the amount of analogue information. Knowledge is created and shared at increasingly accelerated speed. One may prove this point by looking at instant messaging apps and social media. WhatsApp in 2017 reached 1.3 billion monthly active users, becoming the world's most popular messaging app alongside Facebook Messenger. In India alone, on 31 December 2017 fourteen billion messages were reportedly exchanged through

---

[10] See M. CASTELLS, *The Rise of the Network Society*, Blackwell, 1996.
[11] See A. LUPIA & G. SIN, 'Which public goods are endangered? How evolving communication technologies affect the logic of collective action', *Public Choice*, 117, 315-331 (2003).
[12] See G. MULGAN, *Connexity: How to Live in a Connected World*, Harvard Business School Press, 1997.
[13] See MCKINSEY, Global Connectedness Index 2016, available at www.dhl.com.
[14] See WORLD BANK, Mobile Cellular Subscriptions, available at http://databank.worldbank.org.
[15] See M. WINNICK, 'Putting a finger on our phone obsession', *Dscout blog*, 16 June 2016, https://blog.dscout.com/mobile-touches.

the app.[16] As of the third quarter of 2017, Facebook had 2.07 billion monthly active users and the microblogging service Twitter averaged 330 million monthly active users. It didn't take long for politicians to understand the potential of these tools. World leaders have 856 Twitter accounts with 357 million followers, and 606 Facebook accounts with 283.2 million followers, according to Burson-Marsteller's 2017 Twiplomacy study. Pope Francis ranks first among leaders on Twitter, the second and third positions being contested by Donald Trump and Narendra Modi, with over 30 million followers.[17]

Highly participatory at its core, our present 'convergence culture' allows anyone with an internet connection to actively participate in matters that, in the past, were reserved to an elite few (such as opinion-makers and politicians).[18] When considering how we interact online, argues Trevor Smith, it becomes clear that 'the Internet is not just a technological object or tool, but a new form of space'.[19] Smith distinguishes three layers to this space: a physical layer, corresponding to the physical infrastructure of the internet; a software layer, composed of the websites and programs that run on the internet; and, finally, a layer that he calls 'wetware'. This is composed of the people that use the internet and determine the entire structure. Stefania Milan adopts a similar perspective when she describes as 'materiality' the online platforms and the devices that people rely upon for interpersonal communication or organising.[20]

---

[16] See M. SINGH, 'WhatsApp hits 200 million active users in India', *Mashable*, 24 February 2017, http://mashable.com/2017/02/24/whatsapp-india-200-million-active-users.
[17] See http://twiplomacy.com/blog/twiplomacy-study-2017.
[18] See H. JENKINS, *Confronting the Challenges of Participatory Culture: Media Education for the Twenty-First Century*, MIT Press, 2009.
[19] See T.G. SMITH, *Politicizing Digital Space: Theory, the Internet and Renewing Democracy*, University of Westminster Press, 2017, p. 8.
[20] See S. MILAN, 'From social movements to cloud protesting: the evolution of collective identity', *Information, Communication & Society*, 18.8, 887-900 (2015).

6. Increased convergence, higher expectations

Obviously, increased convergence translates into higher expectations. Contemporary audiences are demanding. We have reached the point where government leaders blame citizens' expectations as a key reason for the lack of trust in governments, complaining that the public expect them to solve all their problems. David Schoenbrod outlines five 'tricks' used by politicians to take credit for promising good news, while actually attempting to avoid blame for bad or no results.[21]

But wait! Isn't solving peoples' problems something that politicians are supposed to do? Of course it is. But politics today is not like it was fifty, or even twenty-five, years ago. And the reason for this can be summed up in one word: expectations. To borrow the words of Ethan Zuckerman, the 'participatory civics' disengage from governments and institutions to (re-)engage into individual and collective use of media, markets and codes to advocate for change.[22] Zuckerman observes the shift that has occurred in media production and consumption over the last decade. From a world composed of small professional producers of news, we have shifted to a world where a broader range of the population is directly involved in making and sharing the media. Zuckerman posits that this shift may cause another important change in public participation: a shift in 'civics', that becomes more participatory and inclusive, but also less predictable. In other words, Zuckerman theorises a world in which participation in the public sphere is less about engagement with government institutions and more about individuals using media, markets and codes to seek change.

It is thanks to technologies - argues Gavin Newsom - that citizens are enabled to become problem-solvers in the public domain.[23] These 'autonomous citizens', to use Stephen Coleman's words, not

---

[21] See D. Schoenbrod, *DC Confidential*, Encounter Books, 2017.
[22] See E. Zuckerman, 'New media, new civics?', *Policy & Internet*, 6.2, 151-168 (2014).
[23] See G. Newsom, *Citizenville*, Penguin, 2013.

only contribute to solving problems, but increasingly call for creative avenues for engaging in policy-making.²⁴

Until twenty years ago, before the appearance of the first online platforms, advocacy campaigns were based around postcards, phone calls and multipart mailers. Advocacy was expensive, time-consuming and extremely difficult to measure. Today, technology has multiplied the interactions between citizens-activists and policy-makers a hundredfold. Real-time measurement is possible and costs have reduced dramatically.

In the categorisation of different types of internet politics proposed by Michael Margolis and David Resnick, 'Political uses of the Net' - namely, the activities of citizens and activists to achieve political goals through the use of internet - have surpassed both 'politics that affect the Net' and 'politics within the Net'.²⁵ Technologies, and the internet in particular, can be portrayed as a platform for both corporate and subversive activity, argue Alexander Galloway and Eugene Thacker. The internet's structure, both highly centralised and dispersed, makes it an ideal platform for a broad range of civic and political activities.²⁶ Archon Fung, Hollie Russon Gilman and Jennifer Shkabatur concur. They classify six impacts of digital innovations—internet in particular—on civil society. These impacts include the way digital technologies help citizens to engage directly with political elites, and the way they enable interest groups to shape public opinion and mobilise their constituents.²⁷

Technological progress has allowed citizens to interact via net-

---

[24] See S. Coleman, 'Doing IT for themselves: management versus autonomy in youth e-citizenship' in W.L. Bennett (ed.), *Civic Life Online: Learning How Digital Media Can Engage Youth*, MIT Press, 2008.
[25] See M. Margolis & D. Resnick, *Politics as Usual: The Cyberspace Revolution*, Sage, 2000.
[26] See A. Galloway & E. Thacker, *The Exploit: A Theory of Networks*, University of Minnesota Press 2007.
[27] See A. Fung, H. Russon Gilman & J. Shkabatur, 'Six models for the internet + politics', *International Studies Review*, 15, 30-47 (2013).

works, reciprocate favours, build trust, engage in 'connective action',[28] and eventually turn into 'communities of practice' or 'trust communities'. Connection is key to define contemporary citizens— the *cinquième pouvoir* (Fifth Estate), in the words of Thierry Crouzet.[29] As Jean Lave and Etienne Wenger explain, communities of practice identify the common social situation around which people collaborate to develop ideas.[30] Irene Wu elaborates on this further. She explains that, progressively, the information and ideas exchanged through the internet by members of trust communities become key sources of power. Trust communities convey different ideas and information that, in a later stage, are advocated towards established powers.[31] Increased citizen voice against elite power and bureaucratic rationality - add Caroline Lee, Michael McQuarrie and Edward Walker - has started a 'participatory revolution'.[32]

7. Escaping anachronism

Needless to say, public regulators have struggled to adapt to these changes. Fifty years ago, Arthur Stinchcombe coined the term 'social technology' to describe the evolutionary path followed by regulatory institutions.[33] Yet, responding quickly to the demands of citizens and communities, and engaging them in the exercise of public power, remains a complex task for public regulators.

When not openly hostile to innovations, public regulators are

---

[28] On the concept of 'connective action', See L.W. Bennett & A. Segerberg, *The Logic of Connective Action Digital Media and the Personalization of Contentious Politics*, Cambridge University Press, 2013.
[29] See T. Crouzet, *Le cinquieme pouvoir : Comment internet bouleverse la politique*, Bourin, 2007.
30 See J. Lave & E. Wenger, *Situated Learning: Legitimate Peripheral Participation*, Cambridge University Press, 1991.
[31] See I. Wu, *Forging Trust Communities. How Technology Changes Politics*, Johns Hopkins University Press, 2015.
[32] See C. Lee, M. McQuarrie & E. Walker, *Democratizing Inequalities: Dilemmas of the New Public Participation*, NYU Press, 2015.
[33] See A.L. Stinchcombe, 'Social structure and organization' in J.G. March (ed.), *Handbook of Organizations*, Routledge, 1965.

slow to adapt to them. Gavin Newsom gives us an amusing example. During the same period that President Roosevelt was delivering his ground-breaking fireside chats by radio, the Congress in the United States (US) was passing laws attempting to keep microphones off the congressional floor.[34]

Only a small number of municipalities, governments, parliaments and supranational institutions are trying to escape from anachronistic structures and procedures to adapt to societal changes. The majority of democratic institutions, both national and supranational, struggle to keep pace with the societies they serve. As pointed out by Gil-Garcia, Helbig and Ojo, it is just their nature. Public administrations persist with traditional ways of operating because they are not exposed to market competition.[35] The results of this approach are, at best, discouraging. Over 70% of the policy-makers surveyed by Deloitte believe their organisation's digital capabilities lag behind those in the private sector.[36]

Warren Sack explains this delay by highlighting the tendency of public authorities to use the internet as a one-way publishing and distribution network, rather than a medium to connect the many to the many.[37] Schlosberg, Shulman and Zavetoski agree. Public regulators, they explain, are largely missing the potential that the internet offers in terms of interaction and accountability.[38]

The case of national parliaments is telling. In 2017, the Universitat Autònoma de Barcelona published a comparative study of ten parliaments (five European and five from the Americas) focused on how legislative bodies use digital tools to promote participation.

---

[34] See Newsom, Citizenville.
[35] See J.R. Gil-Garcia, N. Helbig & A. Ojo, 'Being smart: Emerging technologies and innovation in the public sector', *Government Information Quarterly*, 31, 1-18 (2014).
[36] See Deloitte Digital, *Digital government transformation*, Deloitte, 2015.
[37] See W. Sack, 'Discourse architecture and very large-scale conversation' in R. Latham & S. Sassen (eds.), *Digital Formations: IT and New Architecture in the Global Realm*, 242-282, Princeton University Press, 2005.
[38] See D. Schlosberg, S.W. Shulman & S. Zavetoski, 'Virtual environmental citizenship: Web-based public participation in rulemaking in the United States' in A. Dobson & D. Bells (eds.), *Environmental Citizenship*, 207-236, MIT Press, 2006.

The research stressed a worrying tendency: all parliaments sampled were reluctant to use ICT tools to reconnect with citizens.[39] The situation was the same with local administrations. In 2016, *Governing* magazine and Living Cities ran a survey to assess which citizen engagement tools were most prevalent at the municipal level.[40] The survey found that many of the cities surveyed were struggling with following up on their engagement efforts. Although 90% of the participants said they were using some kind of citizen engagement technology, 40% said they needed to improve the ways they use that input. And even when they do use citizen engagement for some scope, 41% said they do not let residents know they made a difference.

8. Conceptual shifts

Hence, the question: Why are games being experimented with as a way to innovate policy-making? The most immediate answer is that, in the eyes of public regulators, gamification seems to offer an easy, inexpensive and potentially highly remunerative way of engaging demanding audiences while maintaining high levels of trust in the institutions. Obviously, it is a lot more problematic than it looks. First and foremost, the introduction of gamification in policy-making postulates a deep conceptual shift about the exercise of public power.

In her book on civic innovation in governments, Beth Noveck helps us in naming these shifts by identifying the cultural hurdles that stand in the way of opening up governments to citizens. Noveck identifies three such hurdles (each of those corresponding to a cultural shift). The first is the 'myth of spectator citizenship'. This is the belief that only professional public servants possess the requisites

---

[39] See S.G. LUQUE, I. VILLEGAS SIMON & T. DURAN BECERRA, 'Use of the websites of parliaments to promote citizen deliberation in the process of public decision-making: Comparative study of ten countries', *Communication & Society*, 30.4, 77-97 (2017).
[40] See Governing, Equipt to Innovate, available at http://www.governing.com/equipt

and skills to govern.⁴¹ This issue will be re-examined often throughout this book. We will use it to analyse those types of gamified governance that, contrary to what one might expect, are aimed at restricting stakeholder's access to policy-making. It will also be useful in describing the publics engaged by gamified governance; as well as during the discussion on 'capturing the regulators' (Chapter 5). The second obstacle to opening governments to citizens' expertise is termed the 'decision-making culture'. The dominant culture in public decision-making, explains Noveck, is top-down oriented and largely lacking the mindset for experimentation. Nassim Taleb makes a similar point in his book *Antifragile*, where he criticises bureaucratic hierarchy for churning out ineffective decisions.⁴²

Academics agree. Max Weber,⁴³ Elliot Posner,⁴⁴ Eyal Benvenisti and George W. Downs,⁴⁵ among others, argued about the incremental nature of (confirming, in a direct or indirect way, the non-porousness of) the 'bureaucratic culture'. A third impediment identified by Noveck is the lack of 'mental models' for the alternatives to professionalised governance. Such models, adds Noveck, would help to create a shared understanding of the goals towards which public institutions should move. In sum, introducing gamification into governance implies a shift in reuniting citizenship and expertise; it postulates a bottom-up approach to building public policies, and it necessitates new mental models for conceiving the exercise of regulatory powers from public institutions.

---

[41] See B. NOVECK, *Smarter Citizens, Smarter State*, Harvard University Press, 2015, p. 29.
[42] See N. TALEB, *Antifragile: Things That Gain From Disorder*, Random House, 2012.
[43] See M. WEBER, *Economy and Society*, University of California Press, 1978.
[44] See E. POSNER, 'Sources of institutional change: The supranational origins of Europe's new stock markets', *World Politics*, 58.1, 1-40 (2005).
[45] See E. BENVENISTI & G.W. DOWNS, 'The empire's new clothes: Political economy and the fragmentation of international law, *Stanford Law Review*, 60.2, 595-644 (2007).

9. Gamification at crossroads no. 1 - nudging

If gamification is expected to innovate decision-making by adapting it to the demands of citizens in the digital age, we should first ask ourselves what type of innovation is produced by gamification in public governance. We should then question the extent to which gamification is making governance more participatory. Let us leave aside the second question for the moment and focus on the first. Exactly what type of innovation does gamification bring into governance? To answer this question, it is worth looking at the similarities (and differences) between gamification, 'democratic innovations', 'nudging', 'crowdsourcing' and 'civic technology'.

To begin, let us look at nudging. In their popular book on nudge theory, Nobel Prize-winner Richard Thaler and Cass Sunstein suggest that nudges may be used to promote (a more preferred) collective behaviour, rather than obstruct it. Nudges—argue Thaler and Sunstein—may help regulators to avoid some of the challenges and potential pitfalls of traditional regulation, for example costly procedures and ineffective campaigning, or invasive choice regulation, such as bans.[46] Put this way, gamification and nudge theory have a clear connection with each other. They share the same potential, and the risks are alike.

Both nudge and gamification have the potential to enhance civic awareness and engagement. On this point, there have been various debates about freedom of choice, individual autonomy and the use of choice architecture. Theorists of nudge postulate that citizens who are provided with social clues or given a direct voice in decision-making will probably increase their willingness to participate and do positive things for themselves and society. By the same token, gamification strategies are premised on the idea that games embody great potential in capturing citizens' attention and stimulating their inter-

---

[46] See R. Thaler & C. Sunstein, *Nudge: Improving Decisions About Health, Wealth, and Happiness*, Yale University Press, 2008. See also A. Alemanno & A.L. Sibony, *Nudge and the Law: A European Perspective*, Hart Publishing, 2015.

est with fun (intrinsic motivator) as well as rewards (extrinsic motivator). This potential is exploited by gamification strategies to enhance civil society actors' will to participate in public decisions. Fundamentally, gamification's inner potential is a successful combination of intrinsic motivations and extrinsic rewards. The former, in particular, are pursued through the redesign of participatory processes in a way that makes it look more captivating, and by the promise that participants may become architects of their collective life and transcend their ordinary roles.

On the negative side, problems with gamification are reminiscent of those with nudge. Ethically speaking, both nudge and gamification raise concerns about the opportunity that public authorities engage in such forms of leverage on citizens' behaviour. Ethical concerns are prompted by the fact that, according to nudge theorists, a nudge works best when the target does not realise it's being nudged. We will return to this argument in a few pages, and raise it again in Chapter 6, while discussing the problematic aspects of gamified policy-making. Relatedly, there is the worry that behavioural incentives (including nudges and gamification) may foster a distorted perception of public powers in citizens. We will have the chance to return to this matter again, too.

Shall we conclude that gamification is nothing else than an evolution of nudging? Not necessarily, not always. Gamification differs from nudges in at least three respects. Number one: the means of influence on collective behaviour are profoundly different. Nudges leverage individual choices fundamentally because it aims at producing a common good; gamification instead seeks to benefit policy-making from collective outputs—hence the commonalities with crowdsourcing, to which we will move shortly.

Number two: nudges' coverage is broader than gamified governance. While the latter is confined in the boundaries of participation, the latter has been experimented to serve different scopes, welfare and public health for instance.

Third, and lastly: while current experimentation with gamification occurs almost entirely online, or otherwise via digital means, nudge is often adopted in offline contexts.

10. Gamification at crossroads no. 2 – democratic innovations

Graham Smith terms 'democratic innovations' the institutions 'that have been specifically designed to increase and deepen citizen participation in the political decision-making process'.[47] The innovation, claims Smith, is consequential to the fact that these institutions represent a departure from the traditional institutional architecture of advanced industrial democracies. Participatory budgeting, Citizens' Assembly, town meetings, online citizen forums, and direct legislation are all classifiable as democratic innovations, according to Smith's taxonomy. Yet, to be classified as democratically innovative, concludes Smith, these institutions must possess two key features: the first is that they are designed to democratically engage non-organised or partisan citizens; the second is that they consist of institutionalised forms of participation, that is, they provide citizens with a formal role in policy, legislative or constitutional decision-making.

It seems clear that gamification, in spite of its innovative potential, does not fit Smith's description. On the one hand, the types of public engaged with gamified governance are often composed of experts or representative of organised forms (Chapter 5 will discuss more on this); on the other hand, gamification is not necessarily meant to formalise citizens' role in decision-making. To the contrary, as will be shown by many of the examples analysed in this book, gamification may be well used as a filter to limit pressure from civic actors, or to pursue scopes that are ancillary to participation; informing citizens, for instance.

Having clarified that, this book does not argue that gamification

---

[47] See G. Smith, *Democratic Innovations*, Cambridge University Press, 2009.

and democratic innovations are irreconcilable. It argues the opposite, in fact. Formal and unconventional channels to engage citizens in policy-making can coexist. There are even cases of democratic innovations, one being participatory budgeting, where gamification has been used to boost the impact of participatory practices, thus contributing to make these practices more successful. We will return to this point in Chapter 3.

11. Gamification at crossroads no. 3 - crowdsourcing

Let us move to crowdsourcing. A recent term,[48] crowdsourcing is an umbrella concept used to describe a model of distributed problem-solving and production that leverages the collective efforts of online communities for specific purposes set forth by a crowdsourcing organisation, be it public or private.[49] The primary general goals of crowdsourcing are cost saving and efficiency. Put simply, crowdsourcing helps organisations to handle tasks that would be difficult to perform without collective support.

Existing studies describe four different types of crowdsourcing, each corresponding to the function that is crowdsourced.[50] The first is 'information generation' (exemplified by the NASA asteroid challenge, discussed in Chapter 3); the second is service co-production, as in the case of Peer to Patent, an initiative aimed at involving stakeholders in the research and review of patent applications in the US; the third type of crowdsourcing is 'creation', and it is exemplified by initiatives like Challenge.gov (also analysed in Chapter 3); the fourth type of crowdsourcing is known as 'policy-making'.

Examples of the latter include Future Melbourne in Australia and

---

[48] See J. Howe, 'The rise of crowdsourcing', Wired Magazine, 1 June 2006.
[49] See D.C. Brabham, 'Crowdsourcing as a model for problem-solving: An introduction and cases, Convergence: The International Journal of Research into New Media Technologies, 14.1, 75-90 (2008).
[50] For a comprehensive summary of the literature on the use of crowdsourcing in the public sector, see H.K. Liu, 'Crowdsourcing government: Lessons from multiple disciplines', Public Administration Review, 77.5, 656-667 (2017).

the e-Rulemaking Initiative in the US.[51] Future Melbourne was launched in 2008 by the City of Melbourne with the aim of outlining the city's values and goals in the long term. In 2015, the city council decided to refresh the plan, taking into account the changes and developments that had happened since 2008. An extensive community engagement process started in 2016. The process was divided in three phases (sharing ideas, bringing ideas together, deliberation) and concluded with the decision of a citizens' jury. The e-Rulemaking Initiative was developed by Cornell University to create an online public participation platform, RegulationRoom.org, to offer citizens a selected area for policy discussion. The aim was, again, to foster citizens' participation in decision-making processes.

Of the four described types of crowdsourcing, the last one is the most interesting because it exemplifies the expansion of crowdsourcing to non-commercial domains, and specifically to politics and the public sector. Anti-corruption, urban planning, transportation and constitutional reform: crowdsourcing has been employed in many areas. The ICT platform Ushaidi (meaning 'testimony' in Swahili) is a prime example of political crowdsourcing. Initially launched by political bloggers to map incidents of post-election violence in Kenya in 2008, Ushaidi attracted more than 45,000 users, exposing to international public opinion events that the Kenyan media was reluctant to report. The platform served as a catalyst for dozens of similar experiments around the world, from India to Mexico to Brazil. In the public sector, a striking example of the application of crowdsourcing is the Icelandic constitutional writing process of 2011. Icelanders were allowed to comment on drafts regularly published on a website and on the Facebook page of the Icelandic Constitutional Council. The rewritten constitution was then endorsed in a referendum (and finally rejected by a newly elected Parliament).

---

[51] For further details, see D. EPSTEIN, M.J. NEWHART & R. VERNON, *Not by Technology Alone: The 'Analog' Aspects of Online Public Engagement in Policymaking*, Cornell e-Rulemaking Initiative Publications, Paper 18, 2012.

Estonians did something similar in 2013 with Rahvakogu, a platform of crowdsourcing ideas and proposals to amend Estonia's electoral laws, political party law and other issues related to the future of democracy in the country. The last five years have seen a dramatic expansion of similar initiatives. Today crowdsourced policy-making is so ubiquitous that, according to Vili Lehdonvirta and Jonathan Bright, 'if elections were invented today, they would be called "Crowdsourcing the Government"'.[52]

So, what makes gamification and crowdsourcing similar? Both combine a bottom-up, open, creative process with top-down organisational goals. Experiments with crowdsourcing, as well as experimenting with gamification, rely on the incentives that collective participation can produce. Expected benefits also include better crisis management and enhanced fundraising for public investments. Not surprisingly, later experiments with crowdsourcing in policy-making included some gamified elements, as an attempt was made to redirect the motivations of crowdsourcees from rational gain-seeking to self-purposeful and intrinsically motivating.[53]

The combination of gamification with crowdsourcing can be further understood by using alternative taxonomies to the one used earlier. Some authors, for instance, base their analysis on the level of accessibility, crowd magnitude and specialisation, level of anonymity, and platform framework and interactions.[54] Following this categorisation, we have three types of crowdsourcing. First is 'micro-tasking in VLMs', consisting of IT-mediated markets that enable individuals to engage in spotting labour through conducting micro-tasks offered by organisations. Exemplary is the case of Amazon Mechanical Turk. The second is called 'TC competition' and

---

[52] See V. LEHDONVIRTA & J. BRIGHT, 'Crowdsourcing for public policy and government', *Policy and Internet*, 7.3, 263-267 (2015).
[53] See B. MORSCHHEUSER, J. HAMARI, J. KOIVISTO & A. MAEDCHE, 'Gamified crowdsourcing: Conceptualization literature reveiw, and future agenda', *International Journal of Human-Computer Studies*, 106, 26-43 (2017).
[54] See A. TAEIHAGH, 'Crowdsourcing: a new tool for policy-making?' *Policy Sciences Journal*, 50.4, 629-647(2017).

consists of web platforms (like Challenge.gov) where organisations post their problems, set conditions and rules for the competitions, and winner(s) prizes. Finally, the third type is known as 'OC crowdsourcing', when organisations post problems on web platforms and crowds engage voluntarily without expectation of monetary compensation (one example being GitHub). Both the second and third types can be applied to understand gamified forms of crowdsourcing.

Having said that, we should note that gamification presents two significant differences with respect to crowdsourcing. First, crowdsourcing, differently from gamification, might negatively affect the intellectual labour of crowds. The latter - argue critics - is worth a lot more than winning solutions are paid. In the case of policies crowdsourced through gamification, this issue seems to be less relevant. As we just said, benefits are expected for the entire community, including those who have contributed. Second, in the latter the locus of control of the creative production of goods and ideas exists between the public organisation and the public.[55] In the case of gamification, however, public regulators maintain full control of the topic and time allotted to participants in gamified processes. This makes the processes of gamification more easily manageable; but it also makes it riskier, due to the higher probability that participants could be discouraged from participating. Chapter 5 will return to this point when discussing the concept of collective intelligence.

12. Gamification at crossroads no. 4 - civic tech

Gamification has a lot in common with civic technology. Bearing in mind that the usage and meaning of this term can vary, it is most frequently defined as the whole of technologies that are implemented by social designers and technologists to empower citizens to develop

---

[55] See BRABHAM, 'Crowdsourcing as a model for problem-solving', 75.

public goods and to share resources, or more generally to help to make public institutions more accessible and effective.[56] Terminological variations, however, exist. The US Government, for instance, uses the broader definition 'open innovation' to characterise efforts by agencies and public bodies to use technologies to access the skills and contributions of citizens and other external stakeholders.

One example of a proto-civic-tech organisation is MySociety, a non-profit organisation aimed at building online technologies to foster participation in public decision-making. Thousands of experiments focused on campaigning, petitioning or monitoring the actions of parliamentarians, or on crowdsourcing solutions to produce social change now exist all over the world. Notable examples of civic tech include the petitioning platform Change.org; Socrata (a company aimed at promoting government data availability and transparency); Localocracy (a web-based tool aimed at encouraging civic participation in local decision-making); SeeClickandFix (request and work management app that bridges residents with their local governments); Carticipe (a French map-based platform that involves citizens in designing the places where they live, and propose ideas for town planning and urban life); and Funky Citizens (a Romanian online advocacy tool focused on engaging young citizens in accountability initiatives).

A well-known classification of civic tech distinguishes between 'conformist', 'reformist' and 'transformist' projects.[57] Conformist projects conform to existing power dynamics, and simply digitise the existing world. Civic tech projects that improve the status quo may be considered reformists. Finally, a transformist civic tech project is

---

[56] See, for instance, A. CHOPRA, *Winning the Future Through Open Innovation: A Progress Report on Our Open Government Initiative*, Executive Office of the President, 2011; EXECUTIVE OFFICE OF THE PRESIDENT, *Third Open Government Action Plan for the United States of America*, 2015. See also GOVERNMENT ACCOUNTABILITY OFFICE—UNITED STATES, *Open Innovation. Practices to Engage Citizens and Effectively Implement Federal Initiatives*, Report GAO-17-14, 2016.
[57] See M. STEMPECK, 'Towards a taxonomy of civic technology', 27 April 2016, *Microsoft Blogs*, https://blogs.microsoft.com/on-the-issues/2016/04/27/towards-taxonomy-civic-technology.

the one that helps shifting power relationships from the few to the many. All things being equal, we may include experiments in gamification by public regulators in the second category, and occasionally in the third one. Public powers may be interested in reforming existing procedures and will therefore introduce gamified elements to achieve such an aim; or may be concerned with enhancing participation in policy-making and will consequently attempt to use gamified elements to attract participants and gather their knowledge and expertise.

A further set of similarities between gamification and civic tech are evidenced by the categorisation of civic tech companies made by the philanthropic investment firm Omidyar Network. This identifies three types of civic tech. The first is 'citizen to citizen' and concerns technologies aimed at improving citizen mobilisation or improving connections between citizens. A well-known example of this category is Votizen, an initiative aimed at connecting American voters with elected representatives. The second is 'citizen to government' and includes technologies aimed at improving the frequency or quality of interaction between citizens and government. Parlement et Citoyens is a good example. Launched in 2013 by the French civil society organisation (CSO) Cap Collectif, it aims at bringing together representatives and citizens to discuss policy issues and crowdsource legislation. The third is 'government technology' and labels all innovative technology solutions that make governments more efficient and effective at service delivery.

The dynamics that run the second and third type can also be found in current gamification strategies implemented by regulators. Gamified governance, on the one hand, is aimed at offering citizens the opportunity to become co-producers of public policies (a concept that Chapter 5 will explain using the notion of 'prosumerism') and, on the other hand, aims at enhancing effectiveness in delivering public services.

If a difference exists between gamification and civic tech, it is profitability. Until five years ago civic tech seemed to be extremely profitable, as shown by the significant growth in venture capital for civic tech initiatives. In 2013, the Knight Foundation reported that the civic tech field in the United Kingdom (UK) grew at an annual rate of 23% from 2008 to 2013.[58] The same study reported that civic crowdfunding projects were, on average, two years old, while the average age of organisations in the most mature clusters—voting, public decision-making, and visualisation and mapping—was five to seven years. In a 2016 report, the Omidyar Network reported that between 2013 to 2015 in the US there was $870 million in venture capital funding for civic tech projects, totalling a 119% increase.[59]

Since 2013 the civic tech ecosystem has entered a phase of shortfall, followed by restructuration, but remains profitable.[60] In contrast, there is no evidence of financial profitability of gamification when this is experimented with in the public sector. In fact, the opposite is true. Later in this chapter, fiscal austerity will be indicated as a likely reason for the expansion of gamified governance.

13. The era of disbelief

The preceding paragraphs explain why public regulators struggle to innovate at a pace that corresponds to the demands and expectations of citizens. The consequences are there for all to see: public services are under severe strain, with public regulators facing increased disaffection by large parts of society. This brings us to the second key motivation for the use of gamification in public governance: the relationship between public power and trust.

---

[58] See KNIGHT FOUNDATION, *The Emergence of Civic Tech: Investments in a Growing Field*, 2013, www.knightfoundation.org/media/uploads/publication_pdfs/knight-civic-tech.pdf.
[59] See OMIDYAR NETWORK AND PURPOSE, Engines of Change. *What civic tech can learn from social movements*, 2016, http://enginesofchange.omidyar.com.
[60] See R. GHORAYEB & M. SOULE, *Can Civic Tech Save Democracy? How Technology is Renewing Civic Engagement*, BNP Paribas, 2017.

When addressing trust in public authorities, we refer to the fundamentals of political theory. Confucius once remarked that rulers need three resources: weapons, food and trust. If a ruler can't hold to all three, he should give up the weapons first and the food next but should hold on to trust to the end. 'Without trust', explained Confucius, 'we cannot stand'. This is the function that captivating and fun-designed policies are expected to play: to let governments to stand.

Unfortunately for public regulators, this is an uphill battle. The powerful slogan coined by French students during the civil unrest that swept France in 1968, '*Je participe, tu participes, il participe, nous participons, vous participez, ils profitent*', is back in fashion. Data on political participation and engagement show a worrying trend of decreased trust in political and (interest in) civic life. Approval ratings for democratic institutions are at near-record lows in several countries. In the opinion of Colin Hay, the word 'politics' is so underesteemed that it is often used as a term of derision.[61] Analysts consider this 'democratic recession', as Larry Diamond called it,[62] the new reality of democracies, rather than a momentary disruption of existing patterns. We have entered 'the era of disbelief', to quote a famous *Washington Post* article.[63]

Already in the 1940s, researchers at Columbia University and the University of Michigan published worrying results about the average citizen's knowledge of politics. Since 1970, voter turnout in Organisation for Economic Co-operation and Development (OECD) countries has decreased by an average of 8%. In 1975 Michel Crozier, Samuel Huntington and Joji Watanuki published a report on the disaffection in European, American and Japanese democracies.

---

[61] See C. HAY, *Why We Hate Politics*, Polity Press, 2007.
[62] See L. DIAMOND, 'Facing up to democratic recession', *Journal of Democracy*, 26 (2015).
[63] See ROBERT J. SAMUELSON, We entered the era of disbelief, Washington Post, February 26 2017, https://www.washingtonpost.com/opinions/the-era-of-disbelief/2017/02/26/e4fa3786-faac-11e6-be05-1a3817ac21a5_story.html?utm_term=.8410cc0aa953

They argued that these governments faced a lack of legitimacy as a result of the excesses of the 1960s.[64] Since then, all discussions on participation have revolved around the problem of civic disaffection. In 1995 Sidney Verba, Kay Lehman Scholzman and Henry E. Brady published a book that reported a trend that many had only known intuitively: civic participation in the US had taken a declining pattern, and this decline was especially pronounced among young and educated people.[65] In *Bowling Alone*, Robert Putnam reached the same conclusion: the declines in civic activities were greatest among the better educated.[66]

From 1990 to 2006, those who reported having a 'great deal' or 'quite a lot' of confidence in political parties across the world dropped from 49% to 27%, according to the World Values Survey.[67] According to the Economist Intelligence Unit's Democracy Index, in 2014 and 2016 the highest levels of disengagement occurred in sixteen out of twenty countries that are classified as 'full democracies'. In 1995 the Institute for Democracy and Electoral Assistance, an intergovernmental organisation supporting sustainable democracy worldwide, analysed statistics from 1,400 parliamentary and presidential elections held between 1945 and 1997 in over 170 countries. They discovered that since 1990, turnout among those aged between eighteen and twenty-nine had decreased not only in developed, but also in emerging democracies.[68]

Disbelief is fuelled, and at the same time encourages, misinformation. Eurobarometer reports that only 36% of citizens living in

---

[64] See M. CROZIER, S. HUNTINGTON & J. WATANUKI, *The Crisis of Democracy: The Report on the Governability of Democracies to the Trilateral Commission*, NYU Press, 1975.
[65] See S. VERBA, K.L. SCHLOZMAN & H.E. BRADY, *Voice and Equality: Civic Voluntarism in American Politics*, Harvard University Press, 1995.
[66] See R. PUTNAM, *Bowling Alone: The Collapse and Revival of American Community*, Simon & Schuster, 1995.
[67] See www.worldvaluessurvey.org.
[68] See INSTITUTE FOR DEMOCRACY AND ELECTORAL ASSISTANCE, *Youth Voter Participation: Involving Today's Young in Tomorrow's Democracy*, 1999, www.idea.int/publications/catalogue/youth-voter-participation-involving-todays-young-tomorrows-democracy.

one of the EU Member States feel informed about their EU rights. According to Ilya Somin (who studies ignorance of politics) the majority of citizens today could be defined as 'know-nothings' of politics.[69] Philip Converse found as early as 1964 that most of the citizenry do not have meaningful beliefs, even on issues that have been at the centre of intense political controversies for substantial amounts of time.[70] Following in Converse's tradition, Samuel Popkin's 'low information rationality' theory stipulates that the majority of citizens have basic impressions about politics, and thus their voting choices are determined by shortcuts.[71]

Recent political events speak for themselves. Over the last two years we have witnessed the rejection of traditional political establishments with the 2017 election of the radical left-wing party Syriza in Greece and the victory in 2016 of the Leave campaign in the EU referendum in the UK. More generally, disbelief in politics has emerged with the rise of populism and post-fascism in several Western democracies.

14. Regulators in crisis

It's not just in politics; governing institutions are also experiencing a crisis of legitimacy. At the national level, governments are elected by an increasingly narrow share of the population, raising questions about their mandate to rule.[72] Kettl's metaphor, which compared governing institutions to vending machines (citizens put money in, and get out goods and services[73]), has been replaced by the Concorde

---

[69] See I. SOMIN, *Democracy and Political Ignorance: Why Smaller Government is Smarter*, Stanford University Press, 2013.
[70] See P.E. CONVERSE, 'The nature of belief systems in mass publics', *Critical Review*, 18.1–3 (1964).
[71] See S. POPKIN, *The Reasoning Voter: Communication and Persuasion in Presidential Campaigns*, University of Chicago Press, 1991.
[72] See ECONOMIST INTELLIGENCE UNIT, *Democracy Index 2015: Democracy in An age of Anxiety*, 2016.
[73] See D. KETTL, *The Next Government of the United States: Why Our Institutions Fail Us and How to Fix Them*, W.W. Norton & Co, 2008.

metaphor. The last Concorde flight in 2003 put an end to the golden age of supersonic flight. The public lost trust in the vision that Concorde represented; just as they are now with governments.[74]

Research conducted by the Harvard Institute of Politics in 2014 found that young Americans (18–29 years old) exhibit record-low levels of trust in public institutions.[75] This lack of trust was confirmed by two surveys published the same year. The first survey, conducted by Gallup, showed the percentage of American adults expressing 'a great deal' of confidence in the president and the Congress amounted at 17% and 10%, respectively.[76] Over the same period, and geographical area, political parties' membership plummeted, on average, by around 60%. The second survey, from Edelman, reported that only 15% of people surveyed in twenty-five countries declared to have a great deal of trust in their governments.[77]

A 2015 poll from the media outlet Fusion among millennials showed that 77% of 18 to 34-year-old Americans could not even name one of their senators,[78] while only 11% of their European counterparts, according to a poll commissioned by *The Guardian* newspaper in 2014, would be confident of naming one of their local Members of the European Parliament.[79]

An acute problem at the national level, the deficit of legitimacy

---

[74] See OPEN GOVERNMENT PARTNERSHIP, *Trust: The Fight to Win It Back*, 2017, www.opengovpartnership.org/trust.
[75] See HARVARD INSTITUTE OF POLITICS, 'Low Midterm Turnout Likely, Conservatives More Enthusiastic, Harvard Youth Poll Finds', 2014, http://iop.harvard.edu/low-midterm-turnout-likely-conservatives-more-enthusiastic-harvard-youth-poll-finds.
[76] See GALLUP, Confidence in Institutions, 2014, www.gallup.com/poll/1597/confidence-institutions.aspx.
[77] See EDELMAN, Trust Barometer Report, 2014, https://www.edelman.com/2014-edelman-trust-barometer/.
[78] See B. LOGIURATO, 'Some eye-opening findings from our big new poll on millennials', *Splinter*, 12 February 2015, https://splinternews.com/some-eye-opening-findings-from-our-big-new-poll-on-mill-1793845263.
[79] See J. COMAN AND T. HELM, 'Voters can't name their MEPs as poll highlights disengagement with EU', *The Guardian*, 10 May 2014, www.theguardian.com/politics/2014/may/10/voters-cant-name-their-mep.

among supranational regulators is even more critical and actual. Debates on the alleged deficit in democratic values have dogged the European Community and the EU since the first steps towards European integration taken in the 1950s. Over the years, following the expansion of EU powers beyond the regulatory field, it has become commonplace to lament the democratic underdevelopment of EU institutions and processes. Various terms have been used to describe the (supposed) incapability of the EU to be truly democratic, including 'democratic deficit', 'bureaucratic distance', 'deficit of mutual awareness' (between EU authorities and civil society) and 'vertical incongruence' (between the EU and local communities). The same applies to other supranational regulators: all are criticised for their inherent democratic deficit, opaque operations and lack of legitimacy.

15. The odd paradox

What reasons explain this loss of credibility and legitimacy of political and institutional actors? Opinions diverge on this point. Many scholars, however, seem to share the belief that citizens have decreased their interest in political and civic participation as a consequence of the decrease in the attractiveness of politics and democratic institutions. How is this possible? Only a few pages before, we lauded the multiplication of the opportunities provided by new technologies for public institutions to communicate with their constituencies. It's an odd paradox. The same one to which Colin Crouch dedicates the introduction of his *Post-Democracy*, where he describes the moment that twenty-first century democracy is living as highly paradoxical. Democracy, claims Crouch, is enjoying a world-historical peak, one of its most splendid periods; and at the same time, it is experiencing a crisis of trust and values.[80]

Promoters of new forms of e-participation assumed that 'going

---

[80] See C. CROUCH, *Post-Democracy*, Polity Press, 2004.

online' would have lowered the threshold of political participation, with the consequence of more citizens participating to civic and political actions held online. Speculations were made on how quickly dictatorships would have been eradicated and cultures homogenised. Roger Cohen of the *New York Times*, for instance, declared Facebook founder Mark Zuckerberg to be the true leader of the protests spreading in North Africa.[81] Very few voices tried to oppose the dominant technological determinism. Greg Burris, for instance, declared that the internet was just another tool among many for political activists.[82] Eugeny Morozov made the argument that people use the internet for thoroughly non-political purposes, and that therefore the internet is not suitable for politics.[83] Lawrence Pratchett argued that there is little evidence that contemporary initiatives of electronic democracy are concretely revolutionising political participation.[84]

Other scholars, such as Trevor Smith, have shifted focus to the reinvigorating effect that the internet has to usher new forms of radically democratic politics.[85] Margetts, John, Hale and Yasseti echo Smith in their study on the responses to the disruptive impact of digital technologies on politics. They label five impacts. The first is 'denial' (politics that is automated or digitised in some way is not real politics); the second is 'bargaining' (internet is going to transform political systems and solve traditional dilemmas of politics); the third, which happens to be the current dominant view, is defined as 'anger' (internet is to blame for everything bad in democracy); the fourth response is 'depression' (internet led us to a post-truth world,

---

[81] See R. COHEN, 'Facebook and Arab dignity', *New York Times*, 24 January 2011, www.nytimes.com/2011/01/25/opinion/25iht-edcohen25.html.
[82] See G. BURRIS, 'Lawrence of E-rabia: Facebook and the new Arab revolt', *Jadaliyya*, 17 October 2011, www.jadaliyya.com/Details/24512/Lawrence-of-E-rabia-Facebook-and-the-New-Arab-Revolt.
[83] See E. MOROZOV, *The Net Delusion: The Dark Side of Internet Freedom*, Public Affairs, 2011.
[84] See L. PRATCHETT, 'Local e-democracy in Europe: Democratic x-ray as the basis for comparative analysis, paper presented to the International Conference on Direct Democracy in Latin America, Buenos Aires, March 2007.
[85] See SMITH, *Politicizing Digital Space*, p. 19.

where we cannot distinguish real news from fake news); finally, the fifth is 'acceptance' (internet is part of our democratic systems, and these have to accommodate to change, through a process of institutional catch up).[86]

Following this line of thought, other authors believe that decreased political and civic participation has partially turned into forms of 'unconventional participation'. While the former involves political processes, the latter refers to non-institutionalised actions, for example protests, flash-mobs, demonstrations and social movements.[87] Pierre Rosanvallon and Arthur Goldhammer, for instance, admit that the steady erosion of confidence in representatives has become one of the major political issues of our time. Yet they oppose the idea that the world has entered a phase of general political apathy, and refer to the spread of activism in the streets, in cities across the globe and on the internet.[88] The 'small d democrats' that Benjamin Barber described in the 1980s - that is, citizens who participate at multiple levels both individually and collectively in activities such as voting or volunteering[89] - are disappearing, replaced by the 'quiet citizens' nurtured by the decline of trust in democratic institutions. These - explain the researchers at the Woolf Institute - are individuals that place trust in organisations based on their effectiveness, and

---

[86] See H. MARGETTS, P. JOHN, S. HALE & T. YASSERI, *Political Turbulence: How Social Media Shape Collective Action*, Princeton University Press, 2015.

[87] See V. MEMOLI, 'Unconventional participation in time of crisis: How ideology shapes citizens' political actions', *Partecipazione e Conflitto*, 9.1, 127-151 (2016); R. INGLEHART & G. CATTERBERG, 'Trends in political action: The developmental trend and the post-honeymoon decline', *International Journal of Comparative Sociology*, 43, 300-316 (2002). Early studies on non-traditional forms of participation focused on the challenges that blogs and independent websites posed to official governmental and political sites (See, for instance, D.A. SCHEUFELE & M.C. NISBET, 'Being a citizen online: new opportunities and dead ends', *Harvard International Journal of Press/Politics*, 7, 55-75 (2002). More recent research efforts have broadened the spectrum of activities classifiable as unconventional participation.

[88] See P. ROSANVALLON, *Counter-Democracy: Politics in an Age of Distrust*, trans. A. GOLDHAMMER, Cambridge University Press, 2008.

[89] See B. BARBER, *Strong Democracy: Participatory Politics for a New Age*, University of California Press, 1984.

that decide to contribute positively in their communities, often without recognition or reward for their work.[90]

However, beyond such scholarly debate it is undeniable that, decades after the spread of the internet, discontent with politics persists, and participation and social engagement remain low. Various recent studies have shown a continuing strong divide between highly active and passive citizens remains for online participation.[91] As a guide, we can look to many of the political protest movements and parties that have tried to promote technology-enabled experiences of direct democracy. The examples of Podemos in Spain and the Five Star Movement in Italy are telling: while effective at gathering people to protest, and mobilising enormous crowds, these movements have struggled to build stable political organisations. It is evident that simply adopting new means of communication does not necessarily increase participation, nor does it automatically shift the exercise of participatory rights to the digital realm. Even more stunning is the fact that no study exists that finds direct causality between the number of internet users in a country and the improvement in participatory politics.

Similar conclusions have been reached regarding the spread of social media technologies. A recent study led by Deen Freelon, Charlton D. McIlwain and Meredith D. Clark argues that social media are probably contributing to the increased pluralism of democracies, but not in the conventional sense of the word. Instead of involving diverse but stable groups, social media are driving the emergence of a 'chaotic pluralism', in which mobilisation springs from the bottom up.[92]

---

[90] See WOOLF INSTITUTE, *Trust in Crisis: The Emergence of the Quiet Citizen*, 2017, available at www.woolf.cam.ac.uk/research/publications/reports.
[91] See, for instance, WORLD VALUES SURVEY (2014).
[92] See D. FREELON, C.D. MCILWAIN & M.D. CLARK, *Beyond the Hashtags*, Centre for Media and Social Impact, 2016, http://cmsimpact.org/resource/beyond-hashtags-ferguson-blacklivesmatter-online-struggle-offline-justice.

16. The participatory makeover

The problem persists. Citizens might be organising in communities and engaging in non-conventional forms of participation, willing to produce social change at grassroots level, but they remain distant from conventional channels of participation. Hence, gamified governance represents an attempt by regulatory authorities to attract disillusioned and disenchanted citizenry into public life and make decision-making more participatory. More precisely, public regulators look at the re-design of participatory processes in a way that makes them look more captivating (and the related promise that participants may become architects of their collective life and transcend their ordinary roles) as a way to foster civil society engagement, confront the decline of trust in the public sphere, revive democratic legitimacy, and possibly overcome the disruptive populist political offers that are flourishing across Western democracies.

The 'participatory makeover', as Carolyn Hendricks and Adrian Kay call it, is a common trend among many legislatures around the world.[93] Think about the behavioural insights teams and 'labs' that have been formed in many countries. Examples include the UK, the US, Australia, Canada, Germany, Colombia, Denmark and Italy. Mayors of big cities have created policy labs to organise creativity more systematically. Think about New York with Michael Bloomberg and Seoul with Park Won-soon. Supranational regulators such as the EU, the WB and the International Monetary Fund have followed, experimenting with 'Nudge Units' to increase the impact of their policies. Such labs and units are expected to act as transformational vehicles for culture change in the public sector. Designers, cre-

---

[93] See C. HENDRICKS & A. KAY, 'From "opening up" to democratic renewal: Deepening public engagement in legislative committees', *Government and Opposition*, 1-27 (2017). See also UNITED NATIONS DEVELOPMENT PROGRAM, *Growing Government Innovation Labs: An Insider's Guide*, 2017, www.eurasia.undp.org/content/rbec/en/home/librarypage/growing-government-innovation-labs--an-insider-s-guide.html.

ative directors, networkers and engineers are hired to ideate and develop new, dynamic, arenas for public debate.

'In a way that was never the case for previous generations', Aaron Timms argues provocatively, 'engineering today is politics, and politics engineering'.[94] The variety of digital tools to engage with constituents ranges from social media campaigns, to web forums and platforms to advise policy-makers on using 'nudges and winks' to improve society.

Does the makeover work? Albeit some might criticise the notion that the legitimacy of democracies depends on real links between the public and public policies,[95] the majority answers in the affirmative. A strong body of academic work points out the benefit that friendly and captivating designs may bring to civic engagement.[96] With regard to gamification, Juho Hamari and Jonna Koivisto select three: one is 'utilitaristic' (i.e. users have an external goal and the purpose of the gamified service is to make the goal more efficiently attainable); another is 'hedonistic' (i.e. users are intrinsically motivated because they feel stimulated in their autonomy, competence and relatedness); and a third consists of harnessing the 'social benefits' that are produced by interactions among users.[97]

Henry Jenkins, a digital media scholar, highlighted the capacity of video games to foster participatory culture in 2006. In 2009, a study published by the MacArthur Foundation investigated the correlation between video games and their capacity to stimulate civic and political engagement. The report identified a direct correlation between the civic potential of video games and further engagement in civic life,

---

[94] See A. TIMMS, 'The engineers and the political system, *Los Angeles Review of Books*, 6 December 2017.
[95] See C.H. ACHEN & L.M. BARTELS, *Democracy for Realists: Why Elections Do Not Produce Responsive Government*, Princeton University Press, 2015.
[96] See, in particular, BOAVENTURA DE SOUSA SANTOS (ed.), *Democratizing Democracy: Beyond the Liberal Democratic Canon*, Verso, 2005.
[97] See J. HAMARI & J. KOIVISTO, 'Why do people use gamification services?' *International Journal of Information Management*, 35, 419-431 (2015).

especially by young citizens.[98] Other examples of increased citizens' engagement through innovative/gamified participatory processes have been debated at the national and municipal levels.[99] In 2017, for instance, Niantic, the company that created *Pokémon Go*, teamed with the Knight Foundation in a multi-year commitment to promote civic engagement in local communities. The first experiment was run in Charlotte, North Carolina: residents could explore sixteen spots across the city and, while playing, engage in civic activities and connect with other players.

Several scientific reports reach the same conclusions. The 2017 *Governance Report* published by the Hertie School of Governance focuses on democratic innovations that governments around the world are using to make democracies 'resilient' from anti-democratic threats. These include the innovations that are aimed at fostering citizens' engagement, comprising all forms of co-governance.[100] According to another established think tank, the Centre for Public Impact, three elements are fundamental to foster the impact of public policies, namely: legitimacy, policy and action. In the context of legitimacy—described by the Centre as the underlying support for a policy and the attempts to achieve it—the 'stakeholder engagement' is one of particular importance.[101]

17. Fiscal austerity, the costs of (non-)innovating

There are two more reasons to explain the diffusion of gamification in the public sector. The first is fiscal austerity. A look back on recent

---

[98] See J. KAHNE, E. MIDDAUGH & C. EVANS, *The Civic Potential of Video Games*, MacArthur Foundation, 2009.
[99] For the national level, see G. SGUEO, 'Web-based participatory democracy' in G. REDDICK & L. ANTHOPOULOS (eds.), *Information and Communication Technologies in Public Administration: Innovations from Developed Countries*, CRC Press, 2015. For the municipal level, see J. LERNER, *Making Democracy Fun: How Game Design Can Empower Citizens and Transform Politics*, MIT Press, 2014.
[100] See HERTIE SCHOOL OF GOVERNANCE, *The Governance Report 2017*, Oxford University Press, 2017.
[101] See CENTRE FOR PUBLIC IMPACT, *The Public Impact Fundamentals: Helping Governments Progress from Idea to Impact*, 2016.

history may prove this point. The global crisis which erupted in 2008 brought the world into a seemingly irreversible 'age of uncertainty', in the words of Giulio Napolitano.[102] Budgetary pressures, with public sector staff capacity at a historic low, did change forever the recipes of reinventing government. The 'New Public Management' approach went out of fashion. The goal had become to build simpler governments, able to do more with less.

This may explain why innovative tools of governance are replacing outdated existing resource-intensive models. Several of the cases mentioned in this book were born as a consequence of disruptive political events. The web-based participatory platform Better Reykjavik, to name one example, was created in the aftermath of the Kitchenware Revolution, a widespread protest that exploded in Iceland in 2009. The launch of vTaiwan, another participatory platform, followed on from the Sunflower Movement, a student-driven protest that came to a head in March 2014. To some extent, the creation of e-voting platforms in Madrid and Barcelona too was fuelled by the rise of Podemos, a left-wing political party advocating for radical change and innovation in the Spanish political system.

Be warned: innovating policy-making does not come for free. Depending on the complexity of the case, there can be significant costs associated with designing, attracting experts, sampling, communication, and so on. *Evoke*, to mention one of the most notorious cases of gamification (analysed in Chapter 4), cost the WB Institute $500,000. Enhancing citizens' participation places a significant burden on public administrations - a burden measurable in terms of re-adaptation of working practices, on-the-job training for civil servants and restructuring of administrative procedures. Nevertheless, innovating policies may help to save resources in the medium and

---

[102] See G. NAPOLITANO, 'Looking for a smarter government (and administrative law) in the age of uncertainty' in S. ROSE-ACKERMAN, P.L. LINDSETH & B. EMERSON (eds.), *Comparative Administrative Law*, 2nd edn, 569-594, Edward Elgar Publishing, 2017.

long term. Beyond finances, designing and implementing innovation in public policy may also help to meet demands that David Beetham would classify as 'economy of time'.[103]

The problem lies elsewhere. The moment we introduce the budgetary argument to explain the use of gamification in governance, we open up a new explanation of this phenomenon - one that is utterly at odds with our earlier account. Until now we claimed that gamification could be used to empower the voices of citizens in governance; but apparently it can also serve the contrary end: decreasing or filtering citizen participation in order to let regulatory authorities to better bear costs and allocation of resources.

So, it looks like gamification may be used to 'distract' citizens from participating. Remarkably, such distractive gamification seems to exist only in national contexts, not in supranational policy-making. In any case, unappealing as it may sound, this hypothesis can no longer be ignored. We can leave it aside for the time being, but we will have to come back to it later, when answering the question on whether and how gamification contributes to democratising decision-making systems.

18. Regulatory complexity, obliged to innovate

The final reason to explain the use of gamification in policy-making lies in the increased complexity of regulatory issues. Urban, demographic, environmental and digital megatrends have rendered many of the old regulatory practices obsolete. The scale and complexity of contemporary issues are so great that traditional bureaucratic problem-solving is too slow, and not adequately designed, to address them on its own. First, most bureaucracies operate in turbulent environments: they have to be dynamic and adaptive, or they will become irrelevant. Second, top-down, direct, approaches are seldom

---

[103] See D. BEETHAM, 'Liberal democracy and the limits of democratisation', *Prospects for Democracy*, special issue of *Political Studies*, 1, 40-53 (1992).

capable of settling increasingly interconnected, cross-cutting and unpredictable issues. Increasingly, synergies between ideas, competences and skills are needed to cope with contemporary problems (which helps to explain why crowdsourcing and innovation are increasingly inseparable themes).

If we sum up these elements - quickness, effectiveness and coordination - it becomes evident that, for policy-makers, choosing how to regulate is not an option anymore. Public authorities are 'forced' to experiment with innovative forms of governance. In the 2018 annual overview of global government innovation, the OECD warns that the public sector will need 'a major course correction' to come to terms with the uncertainty posed by globalisation, rising inequality and disruptive technologies.[104]

In this regard, supranational regulators are interesting to analyse. Experimental forms of regulation have expanded in supranational policy-making over the last decade. The quest for legitimacy is a key driver of innovation in supranational arenas.[105] As demonstrated by the 'institutional performance model' theorised by Kenneth Newton and Pippa Norris, lack of innovation in governance corresponds to decline in trust and engagement from citizens.[106] According to Newton and Norris, it is primarily government performance that determines the level of citizens' trust in public institutions. Once this trust is lost, it takes a long time to regain. Yet supranational regulators' attempts to innovate have been so far disappointing, at least in terms of legitimacy gain. Chapter 4 will argue that such shortcomings in innovating supranational policy-making, might have caused delays in experimenting and implementing certain forms of innovative governance, including gamification.

Of course, the development of experimental forms in policy-

---

[104] See OECD, *Embracing Innovation in Government*, 2017, www.oecd.org/gov/innovative-government/embracing-innovation-in-government.pdf.
[105] On this point, see G. SGUEO, *Beyond Networks, Interlocutory Coalitions, the European and Global Legal Orders*, Springer, 2016.
[106] See K. NEWTON & P. NORRIS, *Confidence in Public Institutions: Faith, Culture or Performance?* Harvard Kennedy School, 1999.

making has connotations of risk. It would be naive to say otherwise. Familiar tools of governance produce mostly predictable outcomes, whereas innovative tools of governance are less predictable in their outcomes, at least in the trial phase. This has important consequences. Being experimental in nature, innovative tools of policy-making (including gamification) are more likely to turn into failures. Additional risks related to innovative forms of policy-making include inequality and threats to privacy. The point, however, is not to escape from policy failures. Rather, as the conclusions of this book will try to explain, the point is to adopt the right strategies to counterweight possible negative consequences of failure.

19. The open questions of gamified governance

We can venture to say that gamified governance sounds promising under four banners: first, it falls within the Stinchcombe's social adaptation of public regulators to change; second, it offers a chance for public regulators to gain the trust of citizens, and thus be perceived as legitimate; third, it adapts policy-making to budgetary and regulatory challenges; fourth, and foremost, it is in line with citizens' demanding needs. What some once labelled simplistically as 'play' is quickly becoming the way we interact with regulators at domestic and supranational levels. Who wouldn't want to have an opportunity to impact on public choices, and do so in a non-boring, dynamic, way?

The truth is subtler. Gamification embodies a number of weaknesses, both practical and theoretical in nature. Put practically, gamified governance does not provide public regulators with clear outcomes (at least, not in the short term). Beyond the promise of high citizen engagement and consequent enhanced legitimacy, gamifying regulatory powers may actually conceal a fiasco. Hence, the dilemma faced by public regulators: should gamification be incorporated into decision-making procedures? And, if so, how? Let us not forget that, in spite of their success and rapid spread, many of the cases discussed in this book have not gone beyond the trial phase. The differences in scale, political contexts and types of issue related with the use of gamification in governance prevent, at least for now, the identification of a unitary and transferable model. Which, by the way, is not necessarily a problem.

Sabino Cassese reminds us that the freedom of choosing laws and regulators does not necessarily imply that rules can be chosen, too. The mechanisation of rules is imperfect. The supply and demand (of such rules) do not always, nor necessarily, meet. For this reason, Cassese considers 'public arena' a more appropriate definition.[107] Hence the interest of this book in understanding whether, and under which circumstances, gamification can be institutionalised in order to have a more systemic impact—or whether gamified governance should be described in line with the concept of public arena. We will return to this point in Chapter 6, when analysing the policy areas where gamification is most frequently used.

Let us admit, even if for just a second, that gamification could be institutionalised. This does not mean that it could also be used to promote civic responsiveness. Here is the second practical dilemma: the usability of gamification as an incentive for arousing interest and enhancing participation in governance. Academics respond positively to this problem. Richard Thaler once argued that governments typically use two incentives to encourage good civic behaviour: exhortation and fines. Fun-boosting tricks, he claimed, add a third incentive.[108]

Styles of policy intervention actually include many more facets than Thaler's tripartite nomenclature. The UK Policy Lab alone has identified twenty-eight ways policy-makers operate at different

---

[107] See S. CASSESE, 'L'arena pubblica: Nuovi paradigmi per lo Stato', *Rivista Trimestrale di Diritto Pubblico*, 3 (2001), 601; S. CASSESE, *La crisi dello Stato*, Laterza, 2002.
[108] See R. THALER, 'Making good citizenship fun', *New York Times*, 13 February 2012, www.nytimes.com/2012/02/14/opinion/making-good-citizenship-fun.html.

stages of maturity.[109] Here, however, for reasons of simplification, Thaler's categorisation is used as a segue into the dilemma of usability of gamified governance. By the numbers, Thaler would be right. Gaming is geographically and socially pervasive. This is undeniable. Games, and particularly video games, evolved from teenage entertainment into a legitimate social practice involving adults as much as teenagers. The Entertainment Software Association reports that 58% of Americans play video games on a regular basis, with the average gamer being 38 years old.[110] The Interactive Software Federation of Europe shows that an average of 48% of Europeans play video games, and 25% of them do so at least once a week.[111]

But, unfortunately, the numbers don't tell the whole story. We explained before that gamification can indeed be used - but as a way to limit, and not encourage, participatory pressures from the citizenry. And while this remains unverified in the field of participatory democracy, in other areas it has been confirmed. In labour, for instance, video games have been proven responsible for a steady decrease of 15 to 30 hours a year worked by young men (21–30 years old).[112] Gamification used to discourage citizens from engaging may perhaps help public regulators to deliver effective decisions, but they are certainly not inclusive. Second, increased use of gamification could lead participants to behave as consumers, expecting fun and engagement as a permanent, rather than occasional, component of participatory processes. Once citizens get used to fun-incentives they may no longer respond to different stimuli, leaving public regulators with no choice but to gamify policy-making. Neither of these options is particularly appealing.

---

[109] See A. SIODMOK, 'Mapping service design and policy design', *Policy Lab Blog*, 22 September 2017, https://openpolicy.blog.gov.uk/2017/09/22/designing-policy.
[110] See ENTERTAINMENT SOFTWARE ASSOCIATION, *Essential Facts About the Computer and Video Game Industry*, 2013.
[111] See INTERACTIVE SOFTWARE FEDERATION OF EUROPE, *Videogames in Europe: European Summary Report*, 2012.
[112] See M. AGUAIR, M. BILS, K. KOFI CHARLES & E. HURST, *Leisure Luxuries and the Labour Supply of Young Men*, NBER Working Paper No. 23552, www.nber.org/papers/w23552.

On a more theoretical level, the dilemmas faced by public regulators raise questions about the evolution of the exercise of public powers in the national and supranational arenas. Two broad questions remain unanswered. First, does gamification have the same disruptive potential of what Charles Sabel and Jonathan Zeitlin once deemed 'experimental governance' to describe nascent forms of governance in the EU?[113] And, if this is so, is gamified governance destined to revolutionise civil society participation in policy-making? As tempting as it may be to answer enthusiastically in the affirmative, we should keep in mind two caveats. First, games (video games in particular) are far from being democratic. Game dynamics are designed and modelled to meet the needs and please the expectations of certain categories of users. Players are in competition with each other for most of the time they play. At first glance, implementing gamification strategies into policy-making in order to make it more inclusive may not seem a smart strategy.

Second, to giving a realistic answer to the question on the revolutionising potential of gamified governance compels us to reflect on what civic engagement is. Clicking 'like' for someone's idea, swiping left to dislike a project, or giving your municipality a five-star rating because it keeps the neighbourhood clean: this is, in a nutshell, the kind of engagement nurtured by gamified governance. Shall we treat it as participation? Or shall we argue that insights from cases of gamified governance means that traditional definitions of democratic participation no longer hold? Opting for the former option is objectively unrealistic. Yet opting for the latter option would implicitly lead us to admit that weaker, or simpler, forms of participation exist next to stronger, or more complex, forms of civic engagement - and thus accept that gamification, at best, nurtures a second-class civic spirit.

---

[113] See C. SABEL & J. ZEITLIN, 'Learning from difference: The new architecture of experimentalist governance in the European Union', *European Law Journal*, 14, 271-327 (2008).

1. What if Government Was a Game?

20. The structure of the volume

In the attempt to shed some light on each of the practical and theoretical problems raised by the use of gamification in governance, this book proceeds in consequential steps. The exposition will be voluntarily non-technical, in order to reach a broad audience, including those who have little familiarity with public policy theory or game-theoretic reasoning. The following chapter will review the landscape of gamification, and provide examples of its application within several sectors, including business companies, civic organisations, media outlets and universities. Chapters 3 and 4 of this book shift the focus to the analysis of gamification in national and supranational governance, respectively. As emphasised in the preceding discussion, gamification is ubiquitous. It is experimented on small (local administrations), medium (national governments) and large scales (supranational regulators). Chapter 3 will introduce examples of gamified public policies experimented by national regulators worldwide. Chapter 4 will analyse the peculiarities of gamification used by supranational regulators. Both chapters present nomenclatures of gamification types, modelled on the case studies analysed.

On the topic of case studies: the empirical examples discussed in this book are mined for very specific points. First, they were chosen to illustrate the various aspects of gamified governance, in a number of issue areas, including urbanism, aid to development, education and cooperation. Second, cases are selected to illustrate the different outcomes of gamification in policy-making. Third, as just said, they were used to build a preliminary taxonomy of gamification according to its effects and uses. The empirical examples include both successful and unsuccessful efforts by public regulators to 'gamify' their policies, where success is determined by the following variants: the number of people involved, the duration of the experiment of gamification, the level of complexity and the regulatory aims associated with the games. As for national regulators, a total of eleven cases are covered. Chapter 4 analyses twenty-one examples from fourteen supranational regulators.

Building on Chapters 3 and 4, the fifth and sixth chapters venture beyond the empirical analysis to address the impact of gamification strategies on the exercise of public power in domestic and supranational contexts. To begin, Chapter 5 analyses the three main typologies of publics that are (potentially) engaged through gamified public policies—namely: 'policy-entrepreneurs', 'citizen-activists' and 'citizen-lobbyists'. Depending on the typology of participants in gamified public policies, public regulators may experience benefits or drawbacks. To simplify a complex argument, gamification may impact on the quality of public policies, benefiting from the interactions established between policy-makers and citizens-players. Drawbacks, in turn, may include the 'capture' of the regulators by dominant interest groups, or issues commonly associated with collective deliberation.

Chapter 5 attempts to assess the impact that the public(s) engaged with gamified policy-making may have on the transformations of governance. It does so through three conceptual frameworks: prosumerism, collective intelligence and network theory. These concepts offer different perspectives to shed light on the actual impact that gamification may have on governance.

Chapter 6 shifts to analysing the risks related with the use of gamification in policy-making. The first is the nurturing of an elite concept of participatory democracy, the second is related to costs and a third consists of the distorted perception of the public. Fourth and fifth risks concern linguistic and privacy issues, respectively.

The last section of this book hosts a few conclusive remarks. These consist of a report on the ongoing efforts of academics, policy-makers, activists and practitioners to solve the risks reported in Chapter 5. Obviously, the purpose of this conclusive section is not to promote the idea that issues of gamified governance are just temporary, and about to be solved. Rather, the goal is to say something about what civic engineers, scholars and policy-makers propose to make of gamification in its current form— a tool for improving democracy.

2. A Cursory Investigation into Gamification

This chapter provides a cursory investigation of the uses of gamification in sectors as diverse as political communication, business companies, civil society advocacy, media outlets and academic research.

Cumulatively, the gamified experiences described in this chapter serve two objectives. First, they substantiate the various facets of gamification. Fun elements, this chapter demonstrates, may serve very different scopes and target different types of actors. Gamification can be used to persuade the electorate to vote for a candidate; it may help journalists spread information; or even be employed to support fundraising campaigns from non-profits. Hence, the second goal of this chapter: to evidence how, in spite of the differences of contexts and targets, gamification is based on the same principles. First and foremost are obviously fun and engaging design elements, such as scoreboards and rankings. Also important are the elements determining the duration of the gamified experience, and the degree of innovation that gamification introduces with respect to previous practices and standards.

The same principles - design, duration and degree of innovation - will be analysed in Chapters 3 and 4 in relation to the use of gamification in national and supranational policy-making contexts.

1. Gamification in political communication

In Chapter 1, two reasons that were mentioned as motivations for public regulators to experiment with gamification were a lack of trust in governing authorities and disillusionment with politics. So, it makes sense to begin this chapter by observing how gamification has developed in political communication.

There is no shortage of examples. One of the most renowned cases is the *Howard Dean for Iowa Game*, the first official video game commissioned in the history of presidential elections in the US.[1] Players in the game earned points for virtual sign-waving, door-to-door canvassing and pamphleteering. In 2004, the Illinois House Republicans released a game designed to represent their political positions on several policy issues at the centre of that year's legislative election. The game was called *Take Back Illinois* and engaged users on key topics such as economic development, health care and education.[2] In the days leading up to Barack Obama's inauguration as president of the US, his team asked American citizens to vote for whichever issue they cared about most on a platform called Change.gov. The idea was to crowdsource from American citizens the priority issues they wanted Obama to focus on as president. Several years later, in the lead up to the 2016 Democratic National Convention in Philadelphia, Hillary Clinton's campaign team launched a new app designed to gamify the campaigning process. The app, inspired by the Facebook game *Farmville*, offered virtual badges and real-life prizes for activities such as sharing promotional videos through social networks.

All these cases had a precise scope: to engage voters. There are, however, certain experiments of gamification applied to post-voting political environments. In such cases, gamification is used either to

---

[1] See I. BOGOST, 'Video games go to Washington: The story behind *The Howard Dean for Iowa Game*, *Electronic Book Review*, 9 April 2008. The game is available at www.deanforamericagame.com.
[2] See I. BOGOST, 'The rhetoric of video games' in K. SALEN (ed.), *The Ecology of Games: Connecting Youth, Games, and Learning*, MIT Press, 2008, p. 130.

provoke thought and discussion, or to coordinate the activities of the network of volunteers revolving around a political party. *SAM* is a good example of the first type. It consists of an artificial intelligence chatbot that simulates a New Zealander virtual politician who interacts with users through Facebook Messenger. Under the slogan 'You can talk to me anytime, anywhere', *SAM* claims to make decisions without bias, based on facts and opinions, and commits to never knowingly lie or misrepresent facts.

The web platform used by the Italian political party Five Star Movement, known as Rousseau, includes several gamified elements to connect volunteers and supporters with elected representatives in the movement. The platform is divided into areas, embedding three different informational flows: a top-down flow (users discuss the bills that are currently being proposed by the movement at all levels of government); a bottom-up flow (where draft bills that elected representatives of the party would like to advance in legislative assemblies are discussed and voted on by the users of the platform); and an horizontal flow (as in the case of the e-learning platform).[3] Gamified elements include the voting system, rankings for the most-voted ideas and weekly notifications sent to the users of the platform, aimed at motivating and engaging them.

2. The politicisation of games

Beyond the gamification of political communication, the politicisation of games is a matter of growing importance. Let's take a quick look at some interesting examples. *The Good, The Bad and The Accountant* was created by Journalism++, a communication agency, in 2017. Players impersonate the general manager of a large city, and face choices concerning urban development. The game's scope is to

---

[3] For an up-to-date analysis of Rousseau, see the blog edited by Marco Deseriis (Northeastern University) at www.scalingdemocracy.net.

teach journalists and their audience about the intricacies of corruption in local budgets. The choices that players have to make throughout the game can involve active or passive forms of corruption. Players are 'forced' to realise that corruption is a systemic issue and that simply refusing it will not lead to its eradication, because this may cause conflicts with other stakeholders. Albeit educational in its purpose, the game also aims at raising awareness among journalists and the public about corruption in politics and the public sector.

Kleptocrat is one of many anti-corruption games. Freely available on the Apple Store and designed by a private investigator and a professor in attractive design, *Kleptocrat* lets players impersonate a corrupt politician who has to make as many bribes as possible without being caught by the Investigator. Each level on *Kleptocrat* begins with a bribe. Examples include keeping a casino open in exchange for free chips or arranging a government contract for the mobile phone company that just hired your 16-year-old daughter as a 'consultant'. Players accumulate points while they establish a network of offshore lawyers, enjoy the money earned, and escape arrest.

Another really interesting case is *Kamergotchi*, an app created by the Dutch television show *Zondag met Lubach* to connect Dutch citizens with the politicians running for the 2017 national elections. The app, freely available to Apple and Android phones, replicates the *Tamagotchi*, a digital pet from the 1990s. Differently from the latter, however, in *Kamergotchi* players take care of a Dutch politician (selected among the nineteen available). Those who were able to keep their politician alive up to the election game would win tickets for the show.

However, it is vital to remember that politicized games do not just tell us success stories. In 2016, Apple removed *Liyla and The Shadows of War* from the Apple Store because it judged it too political. Apple claimed that the game should be re-categorised from 'Games' to 'News'. In *Liyla* players impersonate a father trying to protect his daughter from real-life events from the Gaza conflict.

2. A Cursory Investigation into Gamification

This is not the first time that Apple has judged a game too political to be advertised or sold on its platforms. In 2013, it removed from iTunes a game called *Sweatshop*. The game focused on exploited labour in the fashion manufacturing industry.

And finally, there are cases of gamified platforms originally ideated for political use and later transformed into advocacy tools. Such is the case of NationBuilder. In origin this platform - describing itself as 'the world's first operating system for community and end-to-end platform that runs your whole site' - was developed as a tool to build and organise political parties. Over time, however, civil society actors have used the platform to organise events, gather donations and to engage people with petitions.

3. Gamification and the business sector

Although this book focuses on gamification in policy-making, it would be unfair not to mention the use of gamification in the private sector. Business is the sector in which gamification has developed the most. A brief glance at the data confirms this. In 2012, Gartner forecasted that, by 2015, half of innovation processes managed by private organisations would be gamified. In the following year, 70% of the companies surveyed by Forbes Global 2000 declared that they were planning to use gamification for marketing and customer retention.

After years of experimentation, companies like Facebook have routinised ways to engage their communities through gamified forms of competition, *Farmville* (a virtual shopping environment where consumers grow farming products and sell or exchange them in markets) and the score-based games incorporated into Messenger being cases in point. Hardly a week goes by without a news story about new virtual games from major companies worldwide. Marketing gimmicks include *Nike+* (a gamified running app intended to encourage runners to compete and providing motivation to attain fitness goals), *FourSquare* (a search-and-discovery mobile app that requires players to check into locations to earn points and rewards) and *I Love Bees* (an online game that served to launch a viral marketing campaign for the release of the video game *Halo 2*, and ended up with three million participants worldwide).

It would be a mistake, however, to assume that gamification spread with the advent of social networks like Facebook. Undoubtedly, social networks pushed ahead the use of gamification, however companies applied gamified strategies well before the advent of social media. There is a rich history of companies experimenting with gamification. In 1896, the publisher Sperry & Hutchinson began offering stamps to retailers and consumers. They could redeem stamps for items from a catalogue. In the 1990s, companies such as Gillette and Sunbeam organised competitions to encourage innovative ideas from individual customers. The case of GoldCorp, a Toronto-based mining company, is well-known. In 1999, GoldCorp had seemingly exhausted its once-lucrative gold mine and was on the verge of collapse. In a last-ditch effort to save the company, the CEO, Rob McEwen, initiated the GoldCorp Challenge, publishing online all the proprietary geological data about the mine, and offering $500,000 in prize money to anyone who could find gold. The word spread quickly, mostly by word of mouth, and hundreds of amateurs and professional geologists, as well as academics, sifted through the data in a collaborative way that the company in-house geologists could not match. Participants identified fifty-five target areas of the mine that were previously unexplored by the company. Eventually, 80% of the newly identified targets yielded substantial amounts of gold and resulted in the company's turnaround.

Gamified contexts have been experimented with by a wide range of companies, from tech giants to consumer companies. If you eat blue-coloured M&Ms, or store your luggage in fancy overhead lockers, you have gamification to thank. In 1995, confectionary company Mars ran a competition to choose the newest M&M colour. Sweet lovers were invited to call a 1-800 number and choose from three options: blue, pink or purple. In 2012, the airline Lufthansa

2. A Cursory Investigation into Gamification

launched a contest to simplify the hand luggage process. The aim of the contest was to source innovative ideas to improve the function of hand luggage.

4. Gamified media

Media outlets, universities and non-profits have also experimented with gamification. A good example is the *Guardian's* Investigate Your MP's Expenses initiative launched in 2009. The British newspaper developed the tool to involve the public in reviewing hundreds of thousands of scanned forms and expenses released by the British Parliament. The project was considered a success and citizens realised that they could provide concrete help to the *Guardian* to expose incriminating details concerning members of the British Parliament.

In *Climate Challenge*, an online game sponsored by the BBC, players impersonated the president of the 'European Nations' and had to tackle climate change while staying popular enough with voters to remain in office. Dutch start-up The Paywall allows readers to pay for online content by providing their opinions on different topics. Questions are asked in the form of an interactive quiz tool, which provides a joyful experience for users, and most importantly is transparent with regards to data retention. Users that decide to take the quiz are fully informed about the use of their data.

Google News did something similar in 2011, when it introduced a system to reward its most dedicated readers with badges concerning the content they read most frequently. Readers could progress levels, from bronze to platinum, and decide to share their interests with their friends.

FranceTV created *Jeu d'influences* to inform the public about the intricacies of lobbying. Gamers take the role of a CEO of a big company, whose main business partner just committed suicide. They have to deal with the media and seek the help of spin doctors to save the company. Other good examples include *World Without Oil*, created by the Independent Television Service, an independent American media outlet, and *Darfur is Dying*, developed by the media network MTV. *World Without Oil* simulates a thirty-two-week long international oil crisis. The game aims at teaching players about the social and economic exploitations related to oil production. Apparently, the game was a success. According to its creators, *World Without Oil* attracted 1,500 personal story submissions, received 110,000 views and was linked to 100,000 related webpages. *Darfur is Dying* was released in 2006 and let players impersonate a refugee in war-torn Darfur.

The boundaries between pure journalistic information and games are becoming increasingly blurred. Examples include both gamified information on current political events, and games aimed at tackling challenges faced by contemporary media outlets. Let's start with Brexit. In 2017, the magazine *Politico* launched the online board game *Brexit*. The game aimed to poke fun at the intricacies of political and national politics in the aftermath of the popular vote that decided the withdrawal of the UK from the EU. In the same year, the online magazine *BuzzFeed* published *Choose Your Own Adventure*, an interactive game designed to help UK audiences understand the difficulties that people with disabilities face every day. To realise the game, *BuzzFeed* partnered with the non-profit Transport For All, who helped to find testimonies of all the common problems faced by people when moving around on public transport.

As far as the challenges facing media outlets are concerned, fake news is exemplary. *PolitiTruth*, *Fake News* and *Factitious* are all gamified apps and/or browser-based games that respond to the scope of informing the public about media hoaxes and disinformation. Albeit with some differences in the design, these examples share the same setup of presenting players with an article or headline and asking them to guess its truthfulness. Players get points for correctness and, in some cases, their scores are translated in a global scoreboard.

5. Games and universities

In the university sector - and, more generally, in the fields of higher education and research - several cases of gamification are worth mentioning.[4]

One important caveat: we need to distinguish between two theories of gamification in higher education. The first regards the entertainment power of games to serve educational aims. Academics and game developers define this as 'educational games'. It is believed that educational games find the right balance between learning and entertainment for the acquisition of knowledge. Two examples may help to clarify this point. In 2017, the Centre for Geoinformation Science of the University of Pretoria, in South Africa, hosted an event to introduce school learners to South African open data on public spending. Gamification was used to encourage active participation during the event. Learners were provided with questions relating to public funds and spending. They could exchange points for hints to assist in answering the questions. The top five groups were awarded scientific calculators and notebooks.[5] The second example is The Publishing Trap. Released in 2017 by the UK Copyright Literacy team, the board game allows participants to explore the impact of scholarly communications choices and discuss the role of open access in research by following the lives of four researchers - from doctoral research to their academic legacies.

Different from educational games are the cases in which gamification is incorporated into university research endeavours. Probably the best-known example of this kind is *Foldit*, a collaborative game-like online program for discovering how proteins fold, developed by

---

[4] For an overview of the use of gamification in the field of higher education, see A. HANSCH, C. NEWMAN & T. SCHILDHAUER, *Fostering Engagement with Gamification: Review of Current Practices on Online Learning Platforms*, Discussion Paper 2015-04, Alexander von Humboldt Institut für Internet und Gesellschaft, 2015.

[5] For further information, see CENTRE FOR GEOINFORMATION SCIENCE, 'Gamification of open data to empower school learners in Pretoria', 30 March 2017, *Open Knowledge International Blog*, available at https://blog.okfn.org.

the Centre of Game Sciences and the Department of Biochemistry of the University of Washington. Since 2010 nearly 60,000 players have accessed *Foldit*, in the attempt to fold the structure of selected proteins; and the highest scoring solutions have contributed to applied research in the real world. There are, however, other interesting cases. With *On Old Weather*, volunteers retype nineteenth-century naval shipping logs in order to create a computable database of historical weather records. Once they have completed a set amount of work, volunteers are given the opportunity to compete to become captain of a historical ship. The project began in 2010 and, according to its creators, completed in only six months what a single researcher would have taken twenty-eight years to complete. Engaging people with game-like experiences in academic research seems to work. Cornell University launched *Digital Fishers* to ask citizens to annotate terabytes of undersea video footage from the Neptune Canada Seafloor Observatory. The scope of the game is to help researchers at the Observatory to gather data from the videos, and unveil the mechanisms shaping the animal communities inhabiting the deep.[6]

6. Gamified activism

Let's finish our initial investigation by analysing gamification in the field of advocacy. Gamified activism, as it is referred to in scholarly parlance, is included in the broader context of digital activism,

---

[6] A third typology consists of the use of gamification strategies from companies working in the field of academic research dissemination. This type, however, is not without critics. Authors warn of the dangers of academic platforms like ResearchGate or Academia.edu. Researchers that publish their work on these platforms are constantly 'quantified' in terms of readers or followers. This, argue the critics, may potentially promote an understanding of the professional self as a product in competition with others. See B. HAMMARFELT, S. DE RIJCKE & A.D. RUSHFORTH, 'Quantified academic selves: the gamification of research through social networking services', *Information Research*, 21, 1-40 (2016).

2. A Cursory Investigation into Gamification

which also comprises 'awareness-raising games' (i.e. those games that provide players with the opportunity to learn about social or environmental problems) and 'activist development games' (i.e. games aimed at teaching players skills that may engage them in social movement activities).[7] Gamified activism is described as the systems of rules and rewards found in games that correspond to real-world action.

Examples abound. During the 1960s, the New Games Movement in the US promoted play as a tool for endorsing social change. In 2014, the American newspaper *Barron's* named Crowdrise, an online platform dedicated to charitable giving, in its 'Top 25 Best Global Philanthropists'. Crowdrise differs from other crowdfunding platforms in one essential aspect: it aims at gamifying charity. Users of the platform create their pages and profiles and match up against other users on a board based on how much they can fundraise. Since its creation, Crowdrise has attracted over 33 million users and raised hundreds of millions of dollars for non-profits worldwide. Another gamified fundraising superstar is *Gaming for Good*. Launched in Belgium in 2009, *Gaming for Good* aims at raising awareness about world hunger and fundraising to help CSOs working in this field. The game aims at engaging online communities of players with micro-donations, to be donated during game sessions. The results have been outstanding. In a single event, organised in 2013, gamers were invited to celebrate a major update to the online game *World of Warcraft*, and to raise money for the non-profit organisation Save the Children. The event raised $2.5 million in a single weekend.

Typically, gamified elements are incorporated in broader advocacy or awareness-raising campaigns. In 2012, for instance, Save the Children included the game *Give Girls Power* in its No Child Born to Die campaign. The intention of the game was to spread knowledge on women's rights around the world. Similar in scope is

---

[7] See, for instance, the Community Organizing Toolkit, available at http://organizinggame.org, a game in which players are challenged with door-to-door campaigning.

Gemma's World, a mix between online game and storytelling experience, focused on poverty issues facing UK students. Promoted by the non-profit Children's Society, *Gemma's World* lets players portray a 13-year-old student on a low budget. According to the game's promoters, 30,000 users played *Gemma's World* and eventually signed the petition to ask the UK government to increase welfare benefits for low-income students. Another non-profit Recyclebank, created in 2004 to encourage recycling, now liaises with 300 local communities, employs 180 staff and is used by nearly four million members. Subscribers to Recyclebank are invited to recycle through gamified strategies (e.g. points redeemable for goods at local shops).

Gamified advocacy has been particularly useful in supporting ideologically driven campaigns targeting corporate multinationals. Ian Bogost defines this type of game as 'anti-advergames', in other words, games created to censure or disparage a company rather than support it.[8] Take the case of *The McDonald's Videogame*, developed by the Italian collective MolleIndustria. This game was developed to criticise the business practices of the fast-food chain McDonald's. Players impersonate business managers at McDonald's and are required to make difficult business choices in different sectors. In fact, each of these choices is not only a business choice, but also a moral choice. Just as interesting is the interactive documentary/game *Fort McMoney*, launched in 2013 by filmmaker David Dufresne in collaboration with ARTE and the National Film Board of Canada. Players are engaged in a virtual Fort McMurray, the largest industrial site in Canada. The objective is to acquaint the audience with the social, economic and environmental problems of that industrial region.

When not directly targeting multinationals, however, games may also be directed against policy-makers. Take *Dodgy Deals*, for example. Developed by the Brussels-based non-profit Corporate Europe Observatory, this game aims to raise awareness of the lack of transparency of the EU-Canada treaty Comprehensive Economic and Trade

---

[8] See BOGOST, 'The rhetoric of video games', p. 110.

2. A Cursory Investigation into Gamification

Agreement (CETA). *Dodgy Deals* casts players as politicians, journalists or activists in a post-CETA world. Each character is assigned a mission - whether it is to pass a law for the prevention of toxic gold-mining or to write a newspaper article about weedkillers - and navigate the formidable new obstacles that, according to the authors of the game, CETA will introduce via 'regulatory cooperation'.

Raising awareness on social and political issues is particularly promising in gamified advocacy. The phenomenon is so widespread that start-up companies have been founded solely to create games aimed at promoting social change. Since 2004, for instance, Games for Change has worked to create 'social impact games' - that is, games that allow players to engage in civic actions with impact in the real world. The most successful case is *Half the Sky*, which the firm produced to be played on Facebook. This game was in fact designed to bring social engagement through this social network. The game resembles the aesthetics of *Farmville*, with the difference that players are challenged to reflect on women's precarious situations all over the world. The game gathered 800,000 players in the first three months after its launch and contributed more than $300,000 in donations or sponsorships.

Highly sensitive social issues like peace-building, social welfare, the gender gap, food security, corruption and diversity have all been targets of gamification. Peace-building is at the heart of *Playground*, promoted by the homonymous Spanish magazine. Players are informed of the effects that war has on civilians around the world. The theme of *iHobo*, an app that generates a virtual homeless person, is social welfare. After installing the app, players are asked to care for the needs of a (virtual) homeless person for three days. If the player fails, the persons' resources run out and they die. At the end of the three-day period, players are requested to donate a small sum to Doupal, a charity devoted to caring for the homeless. According to the promoters of the app, *iHobo* has been downloaded by 600,000 users and has helped to raise £3.8 million. In the field of gender equality an interesting example is *El Oumouma* (which roughly translates from Arabic into 'the mother'). This is a mobile app developed in 2016 by Jihane Khoury, a young Lebanese mother and political activist. The app aims at filling a vacuum in the Lebanese policies supporting motherhood. In order to do so, it uses a number of gamified strategies (such as points accumulation and an interactive newsletter) to engage Lebanese mothers and expectant mothers. According to the data released by the app, one third of all Lebanese mothers, roughly 300,000, already use *El Oumouma*. An interesting game in the field of food security is *CluckAround*, an Australian app that shows users how chicken-friendly the eggs are sold in stores, crowding the top of the animation with unhappy chickens if they are far above the recommended density, or showing a small number of happy chickens if they are within best-practice guidelines. As we saw with gamified journalism, there are many corruption-related games. One that is concerned with advocacy is Semai, created by an Indonesian group of activists called Saya Perempuan Anti-Korupsi (SPAK). Semai is a board game used in schools to teach students about fighting corruption. The game was so successful that SPAK was invited to use Semai in workshops held in police stations across the country. Finally, in the field of diversity, we have the example of *We Are Chicago*. Developed by Culture Shock Games in partnership with two local non-profits, this game lets players impersonate a graduate black student living in South Chicago. The game sits at the intersection of video game, journalism, documentary filmmaking and activism.

7. The gamification of climate change activism

Before concluding, a special mention needs to be made of gamified climate change activism. This is probably the advocacy sector in which gamification has been used most extensively.[9]

---

[9] See S. MAZUR-STOMMEN & K. FARLEY, *Games for Grownups: The Role of Gamification in Climate Change and Sustainability*, Indicia Consulting LLC, 2016.

2. A Cursory Investigation into Gamification 63

Early experiments date back as far as 2012, when Al Gore launched the *Reality Drop* social media tool to challenge climate change denial. The game worked on the assumption that people around the world are misinformed. Players of *Reality Drop* were asked to click on two sections, green or red - the former corresponding to accurate information, the latter to myths and fake news on climate change. Players were rewarded with points for clicking the sections and leaving a comment. Four years later, two American non-profits - the Alliance for Climate Education and NextGen Climate America - launched a game called the *Get Loud Challenge*. The challenge engaged teenagers in talking to one of more of their family members about climate change and then posting some kind of proof of the conversation online (e.g. a video, a Facebook post, an Instagram photo). For each post, participants received points. The challenge lasted fifteen weeks, and at the end of its duration, those with the highest scores were awarded prizes including educational trips or college scholarships. As the authors of the *Get Loud Challenge* explain, the game was focused on engaging teenagers in serious conversation on climate change with their relatives - ideally their parents. In fact, almost in concomitance with the challenge, the Alliance for Climate Education launched a curriculum to explain climate change to the younger generations.[10]

Also focused on climate change and aimed at engaging young people in climate change activism is *Koda Quest*. Players of the quest - typically children between six and eight years old - can progress with their virtual baby polar bear from one level to the next of the game only once their parents have verified that they had been recycling and conserving energy in the real world. In the *Zero Waste Challenge*, people from all over the world engage in producing only organic waste (that will eventually be used in a shared garden) and avoiding the use of plastics and other polluting materials. In 2014,

---

[10] See H. SMITH, 'Can you turn climate change activism into a game? Here's how we'll find out', *Grist*, 1 February 2016, http://grist.org/climate-energy/can-you-turn-climate-change-activism-into-a-game-heres-how-well-find-out.

Grist - a media platform focused on environmental news - announced a game called the *Grist Fantasy Climate Hawk Draft*. Players of this game had to draft a green team composed of an elite line-up of high-profile climate activists.

3. Games, Rewards and the Exercise of Public Power

In the first chapter, we began by saying that games and rewards have been used throughout human history to generate approval of the exercise of public power. Examples from Greek and Roman societies were mentioned. Public powers have continued to use games in modern times. In 1714, when the British Parliament established the Longitude Prize, a clockmaker named John Harrison was motivated to invent the marine chronometer, an instrument that solved the problem of measuring longitude at sea. Several years later, in 1795, Napoleon faced the problem of feeding his troops when the countries he was invading were unable or unwilling to provide food. He offered 12,000 francs to anyone who could invent a system to improve food preservation methods. It took fifteen years, but eventually the prize went to a confectioner named Francois Appert. The method invented by Appert to heat, boil and seal food in airtight glass is the same today. Contemporary public lotteries and publicly organised gambling are also examples of games with public objectives - for example, fiscal gains - in mind.

In this chapter, we explore cases of gamification in policy-making, focusing on the national level. A few methodological notes before setting out the functional characteristics of national gamified governance. First, several examples are used, some with more details, others less so. Second, forms of gamification directed exclusively at civil servants are not included. This is certainly not due to a lack of examples. It is actually the opposite. Between 2010 and 2015 the European Regional Development Fund and the Irish Government funded IPSE, a simulating knowledge dynamics platform to help policy-makers in addressing regulatory challenges with limited budgetary resources; the British Work and Pensions Department in 2012 introduced Idea Street to encourage its employees to suggest ideas for changes in the workplace; the Nudge Unit of the UK government organised play sessions with Lego bricks, cartons and crayons to help civil servants to prototype policy ideas; during the presidency of Barack Obama, the White House introduced the SAVE Award to encourage federal employees to suggest ideas to increase government's effectiveness and efficiency; the Louisville Metro Badge Program rewards employees of the municipality for small acts of innovation, like creating an open dataset; in 2017, the municipality of Helsinki introduced a board game called *Participation Game* to assist its workforce with the planning of more participated and inclusive public services.

Gamification seems to be widely experimented in public working environments. So why not include it in the account of gamified national policy-making? The answer lies in the scope of such forms of gamification. While extensively experimented, these are not meant to foster civic engagement or enhance the legitimacy of policies and regulators. The aim of gamification in working environments - that of leveraging effectiveness of working procedures - falls outside the focus of this book.

The description of each case is followed by the attempt to categorise it into a rational framework. Obviously, the taxonomy at the end of the chapter is purely indicative. Yet it helps shed some light on the different uses of gamification, its impact on policy-making, as well as its limits. Most importantly, the proposed taxonomy helps us to understand what logic drives public regulators when experimenting with gamification. Some of the cases reported in the following pages are clearly meant to inform citizens, with almost no effort to further engage them in co-creating public policies. Other cases, on the contrary, are explicitly directed at fostering direct participation. The opposite, however, is also possible. There are uses of gamification as a tool to discourage, or filter, stakeholders from intervening in policy-making. Irrespective of the different scopes, gamification can be designed as an add-on to existing policy structures or guide the process from the outset.

1. Mayor for a day

Urban management is probably the policy sector where gamification has been tested most frequently. A 2016 study by the Arizona State University demonstrated something that, until then, many had only guessed: a direct correlation exists between the diffusion of a positive perception of civic participation among urban managers and the rise of tech initiatives aimed at fostering citizens' engagement at municipal levels.[1]

Within the broad range of gamified urban management tools, sizes, scopes and designs are vastly dissimilar. The inspiring principle of these tools, however, remains the same: technology, fun design and high-speed connectivity arm citizens with the power of interacting with local decision-makers, influencing decision-making processes and thus improving their daily lives. Think of it this way: with gamified urban management, everyone can be mayor for a day.

Dimensionally speaking, gamified urban management encompasses sizes ranging from a single square to the entire urban territory. The German city of Hamburg used *B3 - Design your Marketplace!* to engage participants in redesigning the marketplace of Billstedt. Players could explore the virtual marketplace, add urban furniture using a drag-and-drop function, and rate the designs of other users. The

---

[1] See M.K. FEENEY, E. WELCH, F. ZHANG, L. CAMARENA, C. SEONGKYUNG & F. FUSI, *Data Sharing, Civic Engagement, and Technology Use in Local Government Agencies: Findings From a National Survey*, Arizona State University, Center for Science, Technology and Environmental Policy Studies, 2016.

game aimed at improving communication in a complex policy decision environment, and ultimately at achieving consensus on a policy position.[2] Something similar to *B3 - Design* has been tested in Raleigh, North Carolina, with a web-based 3D visualisation tool named *InVision Raleigh*. This tool allows urban designers and planners to develop and envision a variety of development scenarios within the urban environment. Users of *InVision Raleigh* can add potential buildings by defining location, height, width and orientation, and observe the resulting changes to the physical characteristics of city streets, shadow patterns and density. By using simple navigation tools, users can see how development or other changes in the use of land would impact the city. *InVision Raleigh*, now in beta, has a stated goal: to lower the bar of citizen participation. Prospected improvements to the tool include storytelling features, aimed at showing residents future scenarios of the city, and possibly getting their feedback on it.

Up to the next level: in Boston, *CityScore* aggregates key performance metrics about the city into a single numerical score. Energy consumption, crime, Wi-Fi availability, traffic and trash collection - there are twenty-four different metrics that cover basically all aspects of city life. Bostonians are encouraged to participate, share data and information they have, and so to contribute to make the score more accurate. Albeit *Cityscore* aims at positively impacting the entire urban area of Boston, it is strategically designed to arouse citizens' interest at the neighbourhood level. Bostonians are encouraged to share the information they have about the areas of the city they know better, either because they live there, or because they work or spend their leisure time in those areas.[3]

---

[2] See A. POPLIN, 'Digital serious game for urban planning: B3—Design Your Marketplace!', *Environment and Planning B: Urban Analytics and City Science*, 41:3, 493-511 (2014).

[3] Something similar to CityScore has been experimented with in Chicago with the Array of Things initiative. Launched in 2016, the project consists of a network of interactive sensor boxes mounted on lamp posts to collect real-time data on Chicago's environmental surroundings and urban activity. When fully implemented, Array of Things will consist of 500 sensor boxes installed around the city. The data will be

3. Games, Rewards and the Exercise of Public Power

One step further and we encounter cases of gamified policy-making that target an entire city. Take Decide Madrid, a web platform aimed at engaging the residents of Madrid in local decision-making through direct and binding mechanisms. Both this platform and its counterpart in Barcelona (analysed shortly) were initiated when Podemos came to power and committed to a more deliberation-intensive democracy. Since February 2016 the platform has made operational a system of online voting to let residents decide about issues of local relevance - for example urban transport or waste recycling.

The creators of Decide Madrid report that over 27,000 people over the age of sixteen are regular visitors of the website. According to the rules of the platform, ideas are moved to the voting phase if at least 1% of its visitors express interest in them. At the beginning of 2017, the municipal council enacted the first two ideas submitted through the platform. That same year, the platform started a partnership with Participa Lab, a joint public/common initiative acting as a bridge between citizens and local governments. The scope of the partnership is to implement gamification elements in the platform, in order to engage a larger and more varied number of citizens.

Decide Madrid, however, is not one of a kind. The municipality of Buenos Aires, to name another case, has used the same open-source software used by *Decide Madrid* to create *Buenos Aires Elige*. According to the city's mayor, since its creation in 2017 more than 26,000 ideas have been proposed on the platform. According to the NYU GovLab, there are no less than two dozen examples of local legislatures and national parliaments that are experimenting with web-based initiatives to involve the public in legislative drafting and decision-making. The GovLab labels these initiatives as 'crowdlaw'.[4]

---

made available to anyone who is interested (residents, researchers, urban managers) who will be able to proactively monitor and engage with the data.

[4] According to the GovLab, crowdlaw is distinct from any and all form of online engagement in that it focuses primarily on legislative bodies. Crowdlaw can refer to the full gamut of law-making activity, including legislation, regulation, constitution and even policy-making. For further details, see www.thegovlab.org/project-crowdlaw.html.

Examples abound. The second most populated city of Spain, Barcelona, has its own open source web platform aimed at encouraging citizens' participation in local decision-making. *Decidim* ('we decide' in Catalan) was launched in February 2016 to allow the direct participation of residents in decisions concerning the city. The preparation of the Municipal Action Plan engaged more than 40,000 people and received over 10,000 suggestions. In 2017, during the second annual conference of the *Decidim* community, it was decided to implement more storytelling and gamification on the platform in order to make it more effective. The *Active Citizen* app, in Moscow, operates in a similar way. Muscovites can vote on non-political city decisions, such as naming a new subway station or setting the speed limits. They are awarded points for every vote they cast. City-wide votes are afforded more points than district-level ones. The more votes, the better prizes, including a breakfast with Moscow's mayor.

2. Design is key

At this point we need to clarify that crowdlaw and gamified governance are not necessarily related to each other. This is important, since it helps us to further elucidate that two types of web-based platforms for participated urban management exist: gamified and non-gamified. What distinguishes them? Clearly, not the structure. In structural terms, all these platforms present two, overlapping, virtual spaces. The first prepares citizens for debate - a function, Richard Sennet reminds us, which in ancient Greek was performed by the *agora*.[5] Typically, this is the task conferred on the forum for discussion incorporated in most crowdlaw platforms, where citizens are encouraged to share their ideas on improving the city. To be promoted to the phase of implementation, however, ideas need to be

---

[5] See A. KAASA, J. BINGHAM-HALL & E. PIETROSTEFANI (eds.), *Designing Politics: The Limits of Design*, London School of Economics, 2016.

3. Games, Rewards and the Exercise of Public Power

widely supported. This is the second virtual space - in Sennett's metaphor, the *Pnyx*. Such space is used to organise the visual attention required for decision-making, and it is exemplified by the voting systems hosted by these platforms.

The difference between gamified and non-gamified platforms lies elsewhere, and precisely in the design approach. To substantiate this point, let us look in more detail at a few non-gamified platforms: *vTaiwan, Mi Senado, Parlement et Citoyens, Better Reykjavík* and *Urna de Cristal*. The first case, *vTaiwan*, was ideated and developed by a group of activists in the aftermath of the Sunflower Movement of 2014. *vTaiwan* involves a mix of online (e.g. visual clusters of participants who agree and disagree on an issue) and offline activities (e.g. questions and suggestions collected through the platform are addressed in public meetings). All are aimed at encouraging participants to reach a consensus on specific issues. In 2015, for instance, the platform organised a debate on the regulation of Uber in Taiwan, attracting 1,737 participants. By the same token, Better Reykjavík selects the top-rated ideas each month. These ideas are then processed by an ad hoc standing committee. The French-speaking platform *Parlement et Citoyens* and the Colombian *Mi Senado* are based on the same logic. The public can provide inputs for legislative drafting, take part in one-time consultations (*Parlement et Citoyens*) or react and vote on parliamentary sessions in real-time (*Mi Senado*). With the *Urna de Cristal* tool Colombian citizens can participate in online consultations, but also notify the government of grievances pertaining to any government department or agency.

All these examples remain excellent cases of digitalised and innovative decision-making, but they lack a gamified approach. The rating system, taken alone, is not sufficient. In properly gamified platforms we find more fun elements combined together. As a rule of thumb, we can say that design is key to separate gamified platforms from their non-gamified counterparts. *Otwarta Warszawa*, to name one more, let citizens submit proposals to improve the quality of life in Warsaw. A jury of team experts and city representatives evaluated each proposal in terms of consistency with the law, creativity and feasibility. The ideas that passed this first selection were handed to the vice mayor. The best of them - fifty in total - were implemented. A monetary prize of around 500 zlotys (approximately €120) was awarded to the authors of the selected ideas.[6] In *Otwarta Warszawa* we find a ranking system, a competition among participants, a sort of progression across levels, and prizes. These features, combined together, make this platform a good example of gamified urban management.

3. Civic currencies

One thing is certain: web platforms are increasingly taking over older and more traditional channels of engagement at the municipal level. However, other approaches are still possible.

Gamified experiments pivoted by civic currencies are a case in point. Macon *Money* took place in the municipality of Macon in Georgia, US, in 2011. The game consisted of a few simple rules. Over $65,000 in free local currency was distributed among residents. This money, however, was locked in bonds - namely, the 'money of Macon' - redeemable for an unknown value between $10 and $100. The virtual currency depicted symbols of communal value, such as a picture of Otis Redding, a native of the town, and could only be spent at local businesses. Moreover, each bond had been cut in half prior to circulation. Those who wished to cash their bonds were required to first find the missing half, held by an unknown community member. The organisers of the game had intentionally distributed the two halves of the bonds on opposite ends of the city, and across neighbourhoods with different socio-economic status. The idea was to encourage the residents of Macon, who would not normally interact, to rethink social boundaries, get to

---

[6] For further details, see R. LENART-GANSINIEC, 'Factors influencing decisions about crowdsourcing in the public sector: A literature review', *Acta Universitatis Agriculturae et Silviculturae Mendelianae Brunensis*, 65, 1997-2005 (2017).

know each other, and to collaborate for a common purpose. Players could find each other and liaise through a dedicated website, or via social media platforms.

Manor Labs follows a similar pattern. In 2009 the City of Manor, in Texas, partnered with the University of Stanford to foster the use of persuasive social and mobile technologies to increase constructive collaboration between citizens and the local government. *Manor Labs* received input from over 800 participants on its ideation platform and evaluated eighty ideas, of which five were implemented. Participants of *Manor Labs* were awarded with 'Innobucks', another type of virtual commodity. The amount of Innobucks depended on the level of engagement. Submitting an idea on the platform, for instance, equalled to a 1,000 Innobucks. However, if that idea was implemented, the award multiplied to a 100,000 Innobucks. Just like the bonds distributed in Macon, the Innobucks could be used to receive discounts from local shops and restaurants, as well as more enjoyable activities, like a police ride-along, or a day as mayor of the city.

4. Where is the red balloon?

In 2009, the US Defence Advanced Research Project Agency initiated the *Red Balloon Challenge*. The game involved locating big red balloons placed in undisclosed locations around the country. Players, rewarded with cash prizes, helped the Agency in testing systems for improving cooperation among soldiers, experts and diplomatic officers overseas. Three years later, the US State Department, in partnership with the US Embassy in Prague, sponsored a challenge designed by a group of international students from six countries - the *Tag Challenge*. Participants were invited to locate and photograph five 'suspects' in a simulated law enforcement operation in five different cities throughout North America and Europe. The winning team would receive a $5,000 reward. The challenge aimed at testing how collective intelligence (a concept to which we will return in Chapter 5) develops on social media, and to verify whether social networks can be used to accomplish a realistic, time-sensitive and international law enforcement objective.

At this point, some may challenge the inclusion of prize competitions among forms of gamified governance - this book will not. Indeed, prize competitions present all the basic elements of a game. Katie Salen and Eric Zimmerman mention three: an artificial conflict among players, a set of rules to govern the conflicts and quantifiable outcomes.[7] First and foremost, prize competitions sponsored by national regulators (and supranational regulators as well, as we will show in the next chapter) encourage participants to compete on topics of public relevance: security and law enforcement, for instance. Second, challenges follow precise rules. Third, the same rules are used to determine who are the winners, namely those who present innovative solutions to a problem (the quantifiable outcomes). On balance, prize competitions may be well considered as forms of gamified governance.

The US federal government has a dedicated website, Challenge.gov, to crowdsource solutions to public policy problems. The website is designed to help federal and national agencies to find participants for prize competitions and challenges by providing a centralised list of all competitions sponsored by federal agencies.

A visit to Challenge.gov reveals a huge range of contests from many regulatory agencies: more than 700 competitions, that have attracted nearly five million visits from 180 congressional districts and over 11,000 US cities. For example, the US Air Force used the platform for crowdsourcing solutions on how to halt an uncooperative vehicle at a military checkpoint without harming bystanders. The National Aeronautics and Space Administration (NASA) in 2013 used Challenge.gov to promote the *Asteroid Grand Challenge*, a large-scale collaboration effort to find all asteroid threats to human

---

[7] See K. SALEN & E. ZIMMERMAN, *Rules of Play: Game Design Fundamentals*, MIT Press, 2003.

populations. Over the ten-month duration of the challenge, over 1,200 participants submitted 700 potential solutions. This helped NASA develop a new algorithm that resulted in a 15% increase in the positive identification of new asteroids orbiting between Mars and Jupiter. Moreover, NASA officials remarked that these results were possible at a reasonable cost. The whole project cost $200,000, less than the cost of employing an engineer for the same time period.

The Environmental Protection Agency (EPA) used Challenge.gov to sponsor the *Visualizing Nutrients Challenge* (inviting contributions to design innovative web applications to help individuals understand the causes and consequences of nutrient pollution) and the *Nutrient Sensor Challenge* (aimed at accelerating the commercial development of accurate and reliable devices - rewards offered to participants included visibility in emerging markets and access to testing services). The Department of Energy sponsored the *Bright Tomorrow Lighting Prize*, to shift from old lighting products to new, high-performance, ones; and the Department of Health and Human Services promoted the *Apps Against Abuse* initiative to create apps that could help young adults address relationship violence and sexual assault.

5. Be kind to your neighbours

Prize competitions are not exclusive to the US federal government. Case studies also include US regional administrations and municipalities, as well as other Western governments.

In California, for example, the *Budget Challenge* merged the philosophy of gamification with participatory budgeting. Californians may visit the website and decide where to allocate the budget, and then forward their choices to the elected officials. Between 2009 and 2010 the Utah Transit Authority, in partnership with the Federal Transit Administration and the University of Utah, created the *Next Stop Design* crowdsourcing contest. Two iterations of the contest were launched. The first dealt with the design of bus stop shelters for a bus stop at the University of Utah campus in Salt Lake City. The second iteration dealt with the planning of an intersection in the Sugar House neighbourhood of the same city. The first contest received 260 submissions; the second considerably less: twenty-four. Participants to the Next Stop Design challenge could also rate other users' projects and engage in debate in a forum hosted on the project's official website.

In 2016 the municipality of Albuquerque, in New Mexico, partnered with the civic tech firm APPCityLife to design a mobile application that would allow residents to track acts of kindness. The app was named *ABQ Kindness* and had a very simple structure. It basically consisted of a visual tracker reporting acts of kindness across the city. In the short-term, the goal was to help Albuquerque to reach the one million acts of kindness to which the mayor had committed as participant to the Great Kindness Challenge (a global raising-awareness event sponsored by the non-profit Kids for Peace). In the long term, however, *ABQ Kindness* is expected to develop into something more elaborated. The new version will incorporate several gamified stunts: sponsored challenges, social sharing as well as the possibility for users to like specific acts that are shared. The idea is to use this app to encourage the sense of community and foster civic engagement.

Examples outside the US include the Cairo *Transport App Challenge*, *Smart Dublin* and the *Climate Challenge*. The municipality of Cairo initiated the *Transport App Challenge* in 2012. The challenge attracted 250 developers and awarded $6,500 to five winners. The idea was to exploit the potential of mobile phones to address some of Cairo's most pressing transportation issues (safety, traffic congestion, drivers' behaviour, etc.). Stakeholders ranged from academics, civil society actors and businesses.

A few thousand miles north-west of Cairo we find *Smart Dublin*—initiated by four Dublin local authorities, including the city and the county councils—and aimed at integrating smart technologies into local government. The challenge consists of a web platform that hosts

3. Games, Rewards and the Exercise of Public Power 77

projects to make public services more accessible, ideas to support regional economic development, and solutions to create effective collaborations and partnerships between local authorities, public sector organisations, academia, businesses and citizens. *Smart Dublin* was launched in November 2017 for a trial period of four weeks. Volunteers (both individuals and groups) received vouchers worth €100, €150 and €200. They were asked to share information concerning public parks in the city. Participants had to locate public toilets, tennis courts, exercise machines and historical monuments. The information gathered was made available to the entire community.

Let us move from Northern to Eastern Europe: in 2017 the *Climate Challenge* celebrated its third edition. Organised by the Ministry of Environment of Macedonia in partnership with the Swedish Embassy, the US Agency for International Development and the United Nations Development Programme (UNDP), this challenge invites participants to ideate smart solutions to tackle climate-related issues. The *Climate Challenge* is conceived as an opportunity for policy-makers to liaise with investors and experts. For this reason, the last edition of the challenge offered to the finalists a tutorship with a company-run accelerator.

6. Participated budgets

We mentioned the *Budget Challenge* in the previous paragraph, an innovative mix between participatory budgeting and gamification. It is worth clarifying that gamified participatory budgeting is not unprecedented. Between 2014 and 2015, for instance, the municipality of New York City incorporated into participatory budgeting meetings a role-playing game called *@Stake*. Players of this game impersonate a character (e.g. the mayor, a youth activist, a business owner), pitch ideas from their characters' perspective and try to convince other players to select their ideas. The game was ideated to foster creativity and ideation, and to nurture social connection.[8]

Similarly, players of Empaville are also randomly assigned the role of resident or city worker. This pilot experiment, launched in 2016 by an international research consortium, aims at testing the deliberativeness of participants to a participatory budgeting experience in the fictitious city of Empaville. Citizens/players must identify and point out the needs of the main districts of the city (Downtown, Midtown and Uptown), engaging as equal partners on issues of public significance, arriving from individual preferences to collective decisions. Several municipalities in Portugal, as well as in the rest of Europe, have hosted sessions of Empaville to test the implementation of participatory budgeting and to assess the receptivity of local communities.

In 2015 Kenyan county officials partnered with LENGGO, a local organisation that had developed a two-way SMS platform to increase mass participation in county-level planning. Citizens' interest was stimulated through murals, a digital bus, a theatre and musical budget-tracking messages. Messages were targeted to specific user groups (e.g. women, youth, professionals) and provided information on upcoming participatory governance sessions and other budgetary information.

7. Taxonomy of national gamified governance

Let's pause for a second and ponder just how extraordinary these examples of gamification in public governance are. Civic currencies, public challenges, web platforms and futuristic drag-and-drop design tools: experimenting with gamified governance is advancing exponentially, and the only limits seem to be those imposed by the creativity of policy designers.

It is important, at this point, to sketch a preliminary taxonomy

---

[8] See E. GORDON, J. HAAS & B. MICHELSON, 'Civic creativity: Role-playing games in deliberative process', *International Journal of Communication*, 11, 3789-3807 (2017).

3. Games, Rewards and the Exercise of Public Power

of gamified policy-making. This is useful to clarify which typologies of actors are engaged, what forms of institutional design are used and, above all, what aims drive public regulators when experimenting with gamification.

TABLE 1 attempts to provide some order to the gamification experiments conducted by national administrations. Two clarifications before continuing: first and foremost, the table is not meant to exhaustively cover all cases and designs of gamified domestic governance. Rather, it serves to draw out meaningful insights from the relationship between a selected number of relevant cases of gamified governance, the institutional design and the scope of gamification. Second, the table is incomplete, in that is does not include information on the civic actors that were engaged in each case. That is presented in TABLE 3, in Chapter 5, where we first describe the types of publics that can be engaged with gamification, and then match them with the gamified policies described here.

In the first column we locate the case study. The central column is dedicated to the institutional design. We shall define as structural gamification the hypothesis in which public administrators add game elements to an existing policy structure in order to produce some impact on civic engagement - typically by propelling participatory processes, but not necessarily so. By content gamification we identify the hypothesis in which game thinking entails the policy-making process from the beginning. The third column of the table is focused on the final aim of gamification. Three scopes are identified: the first, defined as 'information', is used to classify all cases where gamification's primary goal is to inform citizens; when gamification is aimed at encouraging citizens' participation in the policy process it is labelled as 'attraction'; by contrast, when gamification is intended to discourage civic actors from intervening in policy-making it is termed 'distraction'.

Table 1. Gamification in national policy making

CASE	INSTITUTIONAL DESIGN	SCOPE
Run That Town	Content	Information
B3—Design your Marketplace!	Content	Information / Attraction
MMOGWLI	Content	Distraction
The Red Balloon Challenge	Structural	Distraction
CitySwipe	Structural	Distraction
Smart Pune	Content	Information / Attraction
Manor Labs	Content	Information / Attraction
Macon Money	Content	Information / Attraction
Decide Madrid	Structural	Information / Attraction
Better Reykjavik	Structural	Information / Attraction
Gallinazo Avisa	Content	Information / Attraction

8. Vultures with GoPros

The first thing that jumps out when observing the cases contained in TABLE 1 relates to the scopes of gamified governance. We had reason in the first chapter to suspect that defining gamification as a tool to foster civic participation would be conceptually biased. It is now evident that not all gamified policies experimented with by national public regulators are intended to directly engage more citizens in policy-making. Out of a total of eleven cases reported in the table, the scope of seven are classified as attraction, and thus aimed at fostering participation.

Yet attraction never comes alone. In all cases, it is associated with information. Information is key. Can we then assume that informative gamification is prodromal to enhanced participation? Mobilisation theorists would answer in the affirmative. They draw a line that links civic engagement with knowledge. More information, they explain, equals more knowledge, which brings more interest in politics, and ultimately turns into more civic and political engagement (both offline and online). Martin Hagen, among many others, claims that informing can be considered a basic level of participation, even if limited to the search and retrieval of information. Michael Schudson endorses this idea but warns that information alone cannot be the ultimate goal of democracy.[9]

Practically speaking, all cases of gamified governance that pursue the goal of engaging citizens in policy-making (attractive) are also informative. This is particularly true with the web platforms that are designed to foster citizens' engagement. It is certainly true that public regulators implement these platforms to crowdsource ideas and solutions, but these are also designed to engage those citizens who opt for not actively engaging in idea sharing, or perhaps prefer to

---

[9] See M. HAGEN, 'Digital democracy and political systems' in K.L. HACKER & J. VAN DIJK (eds.), *Digital Democracy: Issues of Theory and Practice*, Sage, 2000. See also M. SCHUDSON, 'Click here for democracy: A history and critique of an information-based model of citizenship', in H. JENKINS & D. THORBURN (eds.), *Democracy and New Media*, MIT Press, 2003.

play a passive role, voting others' ideas for instance, or debating issues on the dedicated forum.

The Peruvian initiative *Gallinazo Avisa* ('Vultures Warn') is an excellent illustration of this point. *Gallinazo Avisa* was ideated in 2014, during the COP20 climate change summit held in Lima. Taken alone, the nearly nine million residents of Lima produce more than 8,000 tons of trash a day, totalling 240,000 tons each year. The city landfills are unable to accommodate such large amounts of waste. As a result, they process 20% of waste and the rest ends up on the street, polluting air and water. According to the World Health Organization (WHO) Lima holds the regrettable record of worst air pollution of all Latin American cities.

Gallinazo Avisa was created by the Peruvian Ministry of Environment, in cooperation with the US Agency for International Development, to respond to this critical situation. Ten vultures were equipped with a solar-powered GPS device and a GoPro camera attached to their chests. They were trained to track down garbage scattered throughout the streets of Lima. The pictures taken, together with the locations, were then published on an online map. Thanks to this initiative the residents of Lima were informed about the pollution problem of their city (hence, information); and they were encouraged to report areas with illegal dumping. Not long after the beginning of the initiative, citizens started to take their own photos and post it on the website of the initiative (here is the attraction).

Smart Work, Learn, Play adopts the same approach. The initiative, developed in 2016 by the Austin Public Housing Authority, targets underserved public housing residents to increase their ability to use online public services, especially around transportation decisions. The programme recruited a cohort of so-called 'Mobility Ambassadors' to reach and engage low-literacy, digitally divided, low-income households to make smarter transportation decisions. The programme concluded in 2017, having promoted public housing residents' sense of self-efficacy and self-sufficiency.

9. Speed camera lotteries and melodic highways

To be fair, we should acknowledge those who disagree with the optimistic view of mobilisation theorists. These scholars, known as reinforcement theorists, suggest that digital technologies - internet in particular - only amplify the engagement of those citizens who are already politically active. Obviously, if this claim is true, we should reconsider the explanation provided in the previous paragraph. No need to say more on this point for now. We will have the opportunity to discuss the matter further in the fifth chapter, when introducing the publics that are potentially interested by gamification.

Instead, let us remain focused on informative gamification per se. There are several examples of purely informative gamification. Take, for instance, the Australian *Run that Town* - a game built by the Australian Bureau of Statistics and aimed at making citizens more aware of the national census. The only publicised aim of the Bureau was to make national census data more relevant and compelling to everyday Australians.

Another well-known case of informative gamification is the *Speed Camera Lottery* ideated by the municipality of Stockholm. In 2010, the city council installed a number of cameras in the most congested crossroads of the capital. The camera ticketed those drivers who ran through a speed camera too fast, but also registered the cars driving under the speed limit. In the latter case, the cameras would take a picture of the plate and automatically enter the owner into a lottery. Interestingly, the prizes awarded to the good drivers would come from the fines paid by those guilty of speeding. *Speed Camera Lottery* is a great case of gamification, but with no intent to engage citizens in any form of participation. It pursued road security and, more broadly, was aimed at informing and educating citizens of the rules of the road. According to the Swedish National Society for Road Safety, thanks to *Speed Camera Lottery* the average speed of cars passing the camera dropped from 32km/h (before the experiment) to 25km/h.

The same kind of gamified nudge has been recently experimented by the New Mexico Department of Transportation, in partnership with the National Geographic Channel. The scope, again, was to encourage drivers to adhere to the speed limit on Route 333, part of the historical Route 66. To do so, the administration installed rumble strips engineered to sound the song 'America the Beautiful'. In order to hear the song through the vibrations of the rumble strips, the drivers have to go exactly 45 miles per hour - the speed limit.

10. Incumbent and critical democracies

Now that we know that gamified governance might not necessarily be designed to engage citizens in policy-making, it becomes crucial to understand when gamification is actually aimed at attracting citizens, or rather at distracting them from participating.

We could compare distractive gamification to Ricardo Blaug's 'incumbent democracy'—a form of democracy that is primarily interested in channelling, simplifying, and rationalising participatory inputs. This, in Blaug's vision, is opposed to 'critical democracy', which is characterised by increased participation and empowerment, and resembles attractive gamification.[10]

Admittedly, however, the distinction between attractive and distractive gamification is not watertight. To begin with, public regulators may well use gamification for purely informative scopes. A point validated by cases like *Galinazo Avisa*, *Smart Work*, *Run That Town* and *Speed Camera Lottery*.

But there is more than that, and it relates to the impact of gamified governance on participation. On the one hand, distractive gamification encompasses cases in which participation is not excluded but filtered. Hence, we cannot venture as far as to say that distractive forms of gamification are used against citizens' participation in policy-making. On the other hand, we must admit that attractive gamification does not automatically translate citizens' ideas and opinions into actual policies.

---

[10] See R. BLAUG, 'Engineering democracy', *Political Studies*, 50, 102-122 (2002).

3. Games, Rewards and the Exercise of Public Power

The findings of the 2016 Equip to Innovate Survey are telling. The survey found that many of the cities surveyed struggle with following up on their engagement efforts. Four out of ten respondents admitted that the inputs provided by citizens should be better processed. And even when citizens' inputs are actually used, 41% of respondents said that they lack regular communicative efforts to let residents know they made a difference. *Decide Madrid* is a case in point. It is true that it gathered thousands of policy proposals from residents; yet only two moved forward to be considered by the city council. Out of the 482 Madrileños surveyed by the municipality among those who had not registered on the platform, 11% judged participation in *Decide Madrid* pointless.[11]

How can it be that gamification may be actually used to discourage participation? One reason was raised in Chapter 1; budgetary constraints that limit public administrators' freedom of action. A deeper look at the cases included in TABLE 1, however, opens up additional, and different, interpretations. In the Red Balloon Challenge, gamification seems to be part of a strategy to prevent collective action from civic stakeholders. The same happens in *MMOWGLI* (*Massive Multiplayer Online Wargame Leveraging the Internet*) - a game developed by the US Office for Naval Research that lets players create action plans to respond to piracy in international waters. In such cases, the captivating design and the fun elements were aimed at encouraging only 'superficial' participation - of the kind that would reduce the interferences from participants and discourage their deeper engagement.

Graham Smith is clear on this point, when he explains that exclusion pervades much democratic practices; and this is not necessarily due to design principles of innovation, he adds, but rather to the manner that sponsoring authorities enact democratic practices.[12]

---

[11] See MUNICIPALITY OF MADRID, *Acción de Gobierno del Ayuntamiento de Madrid (2015–2019)*, www.madrid.es/UnidadesDescentralizadas/UDCMedios/noticias/2016/07Julio/05%20Martes/NotasdePrensa/DebateEstadoCiudad/ficheros/ACCIÓN%20DE%20GOBIERNO.pdf.
[12] See SMITH, *Democratic Innovations*.

The reasons for these choices are very pragmatic. To reduce costs is one, as discussed earlier. Another reason may be efficiency, that is, to ensure that the number of participants in a certain policy-making process is manageable. A third, related, reason may consist of the attempt to attract only certain types of participants. Why would regulators want to do that? The answer lies, again, in resource scarcity. Due to constraints in time and resources, public regulators cannot possibly speak to every interest group.

A vast amount of literature has analysed this topic. Beth Noveck, as we saw in Chapter 1, has a definition for this problem. She names it 'myth of spectator citizenship' - the belief that only professional public servants possess the requisites and skills to govern. A study authored by Thomas Bryer, Terry Cooper and Jack Meek supports the same assumption. Bryer, Cooper and Meek explain that greater engagement of citizens drain resources from professional administrative work.[13] The consequence is straightforward; regulators need to figure out which group most closely approximates the targeted constituency, and provide the most accurate representation of the interests and preferences of this particular societal segment. As further support to these explanations, there is the case of supranational regulators, where distractive forms of gamification are not used. This is due to the priority given by supranational decision-makers to enhancing legitimacy through gamified policies.

The Tinder-style app *CitySwipe* offers a good example of distractive gamification. Implemented by the city of Santa Monica in California, *CitySwipe* attempts to gauge public opinion on elements of urban planning, for example, parking slots, street furniture or murals. The website presents residents with images of potential scenarios and, drawing from the Tinder's model of left/right swiping, encourages them to like or dislike options. The case is very interesting and innovative. Yet is seems to prove Lisa Ward Mather and Pamela

---

[13] See T.L. COOPER, T.A. BRYER & J.W. MEEK, 'Citizen-centered collaborative public management', *Public Administration Review*, 66 (2006).

Robinson's theory that gamified urban planning can capture participants' attention and even educate the public about planning concepts.[14] The reduction of the burden of traditional consultation, however, comes at the cost of oversimplifying administrative decisions.

---

[14] See L.W. MATHER & P. ROBINSON, 'Civic crafting in urban planning consultation: Exploring Minecraft's potential', *International Journal of E-Planning Research*, 5 (2016), 1.

4. Gamification Beyond Borders

Having described the rapidly growing area of experimentation with gamification within national decision-making, this chapter turns to analysing the adoption of gamified strategies by supranational regulators. Much the same is true in supranational arenas. In the last ten years, supranational regulators progressively introduced techniques of gamification into policy-making processes. Yet, compared with their national counterparts, supranational regulators have not yet shown a general commitment to systematically integrate gamified behavioural insights into policy-making. Two reasons can be given to explain this delay.

The first reason is also the most important: it relates to the debated definition of citizenry in supranational legal arenas. The question of what a 'public' actually is and the extent to which civic actors are entitled to influence supranational policy-making remain contested concepts. Academic opinions diverge on the significance of the role played by civil society actors in the global landscape. In fact, while scholars tend to agree on the fact that one of the central features of supranational policy-making processes is that they work only by mobilising a large number of public and private actors, from different geographical locations and policy domains, they largely disagree on the consequences of this 'consensual promiscuity', to borrow Jeremy

Richardson's words to describe participatory complexity in the EU.[1] Some envisage a 'subjectivation' of supranational legal regimes, with the progressive extension of rights and participatory opportunities to private actors in the global arena.[2] Other scholars only see further fragmentation of participatory rights in the global legal order taking hold.[3] We will return to this point in the next chapter.

Also debated is the nature of the power of supranational regulators, which is the second reason that may explain the gap in experimentation of gamification between national and supranational arenas. The impact (and legitimacy) of supranational regulators on everyday life of citizens and local communities is politically and legally contested. Debates on regaining trust in supranational regulators by borrowing domestic law precepts on accountability and transparency date back to the mid-1990s. The EU, with the constant efforts from its main institutions to innovate regulation, is a case in point. In 2016 alone, the EU promoted innovation through the realignment of the Better Regulation Agenda with competitiveness, by introducing innovation-driven investments, and with the development of an 'innovation principle' to rival the 'precautionary principle'. Yet results offer no reason for celebration. Of the six 'political tribes' that (according to Chatham House and Kantar Public) exist within the EU today, the 'Hesitant Europeans', summed up with the 'EU Rejecters', the 'Frustrated pro-Europeans' and the 'Austerity Rebels', amount to 68% of the total.[4]

Critical views on the legitimacy of supranational regulators are heightened in a time of crisis, where (perceived) imbalances accumulate, and political tensions inevitably arise. Citizens feel disempowered and find no relief in supranational policy-making. On the

---

[1] See J. RICHARDSON, 'Policy-making in the EU: interests, ideas and garbage cons in primeval soup' in J. RICHARDSON & S. MAZEY, *European Union: Power and Policy Making*, 3-27, Routledge, 2015.
[2] See N. KRISCH, *Beyond Constitutionalism: The Pluralist Structure of Postnational Law*, Oxford University Press, 2010.
[3] See T. ISIKSEL, 'Global legal pluralism as fact and norm', *Global Constitutionalism*, 2, 160-195 (2013).
[4] See T. RAINES, M. GOODWIN & D. CUTTS, *Europe's Political Tribes. Exploring the Diversity of Views Across the EU*, Chatham House, 2017.

4. Gamification Beyond Borders

one hand, writes Robert Dahl, the complexity of international matters 'put them beyond the immediate capacities of many, probably most, citizens to appraise'.[5] On the other hand, the remoteness of most supranational regulators from local communities makes the provision of sufficient legitimacy and accountability through long and complex chains of delegation unlikely. We all know the consequences; a further decrease of trust in supranational policy-making.

In a recent essay on technology and global governance, Eyal Benvenisti exemplifies this problem using the so-called 'Mega Regional trade agreements'.[6] The primary aim of these international agreements is to reduce trade barriers. More often than not, however, they include rules aimed at harmonising regulations, setting environmental standards, protecting intellectual property or limiting state-owned enterprises. In part because of the complexity and variety of the issues regulated, and in part because of the strict confidentiality under which these agreements are negotiated—explains Benvenisti—public opinion has a negative perception of Mega Regional agreements. These are criticised for violating principles of accountability, transparency and inclusiveness. The surge of street protests from 2015 to 2017 in Brussels against the Transatlantic Trade Investment Partnership (TTIP) was fuelled by the discontent of the general public. Interestingly, the accuracy of the allegations against the TTIP was never a matter of concern; these looked plausible, and for the protesters that was enough.

By the end of the essay Benvenisti enumerates the key challenges for enhancing transparency and accountability of supranational governance. Here, more modestly, we can claim that the lateness of certain innovations in supranational policy-making - and specifically of

---

[5] See R. DAHL, 'Can international organisations be democratic? A skeptic's view', in I. SHAPIRO & C. HACKER-CORDON (eds.), *Democracy's Edges*, 19-36, Cambridge University Press, 1999.

[6] See E. BENVENISTI, *EJIL Foreword: Upholding Democracy Amid the Challenges of New Technology: What Role for the Law of Global Governance?* University of Cambridge Faculty of Law Research Paper No. 13/2018, 2016, http://globaltrust.tau.ac.il/publications.

gamified governance - may be attributed to the nature and exercise of regulatory powers from supranational authorities.

Nevertheless, it should be noted that, when experimenting with gamified elements in policy-making, supranational regulators follow similar patters to national counterparts. Supranational gamified governance may thus be used for educational or participatory scopes; it can be adapted to existing policies, or designed *ex novo*; and it can be protracted for longer or shorter durations. In addition to these features, supranational gamified governance can be further classified according to the geographical reach of the policies: global, regional or even local.

One last point: gamification is also experimented with within the working environments of supranational regulators. For instance, in 2017 the UNDP commissioned a game that would reflect the difficulties and opportunities linked to policy prioritisation, resource budgeting and lobbying. The idea is to train participants to deal with complex policy challenges, and to witness the interdependences between policy fields. The same reasons that we used in Chapter 3 to justify the decision not to include such forms of gamification remain valid. Thus, gamified policies tailored to the working environments of supranational regulators will not be considered here.

1. Gamified supranational governance

Barely thirteen years has passed since we saw the earliest experiments in gamification from supranational regulators. The World Food Programme (WFP) pioneered this field in 2005 with *Food Force*, a humanitarian video game about global hunger. Intended for teenagers, *Food Force* had six missions, each presenting global hunger-related challenges. At the end of each mission players received a score for their performance and were encouraged to play again. At the completion of the six missions, players could submit their scores to an international high score database on a dedicated website.

The most renowned case of supranational gamified governance, however, is *Evoke*, a graphic novel game developed by the WB five

4. Gamification Beyond Borders

years after *Food Force*, in 2010. The game allowed players to impersonate the participants in the 'Evoke Network' - a network of the best scientists and thinkers worldwide - and challenge them with real issues of cooperation for development. During its initial run, according to the WB, the host website drew 100,000 visitors from 150 countries.

While *Evoke* remains the gold standard for supranational gamified policies, many more examples may be found, each of which are concerned with different economic, legal and social issues. Let's take a quick look at some of them. *Economia*, a game ideated by the European Central Bank (ECB), challenges players with basic concepts of monetary policy. The aim of the game is to keep inflation low and stable at just under 2%, using the key interest rate. The International Labour Organization (ILO) has created *Business Game*, which aims to build up participants' understanding of starting and managing a successful business. In the case of *Draw-the-World* - ideated by the Council of Europe (CoE) to spread knowledge of the Universal Declaration of Human Rights - players have to draw creatively to depict a world relating to human rights. In *My Life as a Refugee* - a mobile app game developed by the United Nations High Commissioner for Refugees (UNHCR) - players impersonate three characters forced to flee their homes due to war, persecution and terror.

Similar in scope are *Kids' Corner* and *Walking with Mrs X*, developed by the EU and the WHO respectively. In the first, players must protect the interests of children and young people, and in the meantime learn about the rights of the children. In the second, players represent a pregnant woman, their own 'Mrs X'. Throughout the pregnancy, the positive or negative factors affecting the outcomes of Mrs X or her baby are decided by throwing a dice.

Finally, in the case of *Sai Fah the Flood Fighter* - a flood preparedness educational game app (on iOS and Android) developed by the United Nations Educational, Scientific and Cultural Organization (UNESCO) - Southeast Asian children are taught crucial survival skills during a flood disaster.

2. Social innovators and young scientists

Prize competitions deserve special mention. We reported in Chapter 3 on the rapid growth of such competitions at the national level. Challenges, we claimed, can be considered forms of gamified governance, in that they entail the basic elements of a game: rules, prizes and quantifiable outcomes. Do we find similar competitions at the supranational level? Apparently yes, although on a smaller scale.

The EU is the supranational regulator that has experimented with prize competitions most frequently. Examples include the European Social Innovation Competition and the EU Contest for Young Scientists (EUCYS). The Social Innovation Competition is sponsored every year by the European Commission to award the best social innovation projects from all over Europe.[7] The projects awarded are usually very innovative. In 2016, for instance, one of the awards went to the *Machine to Be Another* - a virtual reality experience designed to give users a first-person experience of the life of a refugee. The project proposed to create stations of archived narratives from refugees and migrants to be located in schools, libraries, museums, as well as other cultural institutions.

The EUCYS is annual, too. Contests are first held at the national level. The winning national projects can apply to the Europe-wide contest. At the contest, the contestants set up their project in a display stand in the Science Exhibition Hall (in the given host country that year) and are required to answer questions from members of the scientific jury. Moreover, the contestants are encouraged to explain their projects to a public audience. Awarded prizes range from €3,500 to €7,000. In addition, the EUCYS has honorary awards consisting of all-expenses-paid trips to events in London and Stockholm, and a number of ad hoc rewards on specific topics (e.g. bio-economy, chemistry or regulatory innovation at large).

---

[7] See http://ec.europa.eu/growth/industry/innovation/policy/social/competition_en.

3. Storytellers, innovators, connectors and includers

Outside the EU there are fewer examples of prize competition. One is World Wonders, ideated by UNESCO in 2012, on the occasion of the fortieth anniversary of the World Heritage Convention. The competition was composed of twelve missions. Each mission involved choosing where the six letters of UNESCO were photographed, from a possible choice of six World Heritage sites. The best photos, along with other images and clues, were published on the competition website and exhibited at the UNESCO headquarters in Paris.

Another case is the Action Challenge Awards sponsored by the UN SDG Action Campaign, a special initiative of the UN Secretary-General administered by the UNDP and mandated to support the UN system-wide and Member States on advocacy and public engagement in the implementation of the Sustainable Development Goals (SDG) agenda. The Action Challenge Awards are open to individuals, CSOs and local government. In total, there are seven awards. 'Mobilisers' rewards the team that demonstrates greatest success with mobilising citizens or volunteers to act for the UN-SDG; 'Storyteller', 'Communicator' and 'Visualizer' awards recognise ideas in the fields of media outreach, communication and data journalism; the 'Innovator' prize goes to the most creative and innovative use of new technologies for communicating SDGs; finally, the 'Connector' and 'Includer' awards go to successful ideas in fostering networking and inclusion.

4. Taxonomy of supranational gamified governance

Virtual networks of scientists, educational games tackling social issues, gamified monetary policies and prize challenges: there are quite a lot of cases of supranational gamified policies to choose from. Here might be a good place to present a preliminary taxonomy of gamification in the supranational public sphere and its actual application, that is to say, the range of action, the typology, the length and the structure.

The proposed taxonomy is presented in TABLE 2 (at the end of this section). The same caveat used for TABLE 1 applies here. This taxonomy is intended to be demonstrative rather than exhaustive. Only the most representative examples of gamified supranational governance are reported.

The first column presents the supranational regulator and the related case of gamified policy. The range of action, typology and length follow in the next three columns. Range of action denotes the geographical reach of the policy. Interestingly, notwithstanding the supranational legal nature of the regulator promoting the gamified policy, the impact may vary. Three ranges are considered: global, regional and local. The column detailing the typology of gamification includes two options: informative or attractive gamification. Differently from the national level, distractive gamification is absent. We will discuss later the reasons for this. The fifth column is concerned with the length. Counter-intuitively, the short and long-term labels are not used to assess the chronological duration of gamified policies, but rather its repeatability. The last column is dedicated to institutional design. Like their national counterparts, supranational regulators may include game elements to an existing policy structure in order to propel the learning or participatory processes. This structural design usually does not impact the content of decisions; rather, it aims to engage a broader audience. Content design instead concerns the hypothesis in which game thinking entails the policy-making process from the beginning. Here the aim is to produce regulatory outcomes through the combination of gamification with more traditional strategies of governance.

Table 2. Gamification in supranational policy-making

CASE	RANGE OF ACTION	TYPOLOGY	LENGTH	INSTITUTIONAL DESIGN
UNHCR: *My Life as a Refugee*	Global	Informative	Long-term	Content
UNHCR: *Against All Odds*				Content
UNESCO: World Wonders				Structural
EU: *Kids' Corner*				Content
ILO: *Business Game*				Content
NATO: *Map Game*				Structural
CoE: *Youth Foundation Game*				Content
UNEP: *Ozzy Ozone*		Informative Attractive		Structural
WFP: *Food Force*				
WHO: *Walking with Mrs X*				
CoE: *Draw-the-World*				
UN Population Fund (UNFPA): *Breakaway*				
WFP: *Freerice*				
ECB: *Economia*	Regional	Informative		
UNESCO: *Sai Fah the Flood Fighter*				
UNDP: *Pop Hunter*				
UNHCR: *Last Exit Flucht*	Local			
UNDP: *Youth Work*		Attractive	Short-term	Content

UN Children's Fund (UNICEF): Tap Challenge		Informative		Structural
WB: *Evoke*	Global	Attractive		
UN-Habitat: *Block by Block*	Local	Attractive		Content
		Informative		

5. Pop hunters, maps and ozone molecules

Contrary to what the supranational nature of the regulators experimenting with gamification might suggest, the outreach of supranational gamified policies is not necessarily global. The range of action of gamified governance may actually develop along three dimensions: one is obviously global, and includes the majority of cases reported in this book; in addition, there are a second and a third dimension that are, perhaps less obviously, regional and local.

The ILO's *Business Game*, or the CoE's *Draw-the-World*, to name two, entitle anyone, from anywhere, to participate. In such cases, supranational regulators use gamification to raise global awareness on issues of concern. Not accidentally, in such cases the aim is predominantly informative.

To further clarify this point, we will look at three cases in more detail. The first is promoted by the UN-SDG. Between 2015 and 2017 the UN-SDG led the United Nations Virtual Reality series using immersive storytelling to inspire greater empathy and understanding around contemporary humanitarian challenges. The initiative produced ten virtual reality short movies telling the individual stories of war victims or refugees, one of which, *Clouds Over Sidra*, was presented at the 2015 World Economic Forum in Davos. The nine-minute film shows the life of Sidra, o 12-year-old Syrian child living in a refugee camp in Jordan. With the second example we remain in the UN framework. The United Nations Environment

4. Gamification Beyond Borders

Programme (UNEP) educates young children about the consequences of ozone depletion through a video (translated into twenty-two languages), several comic books, a dedicated website, and of course an online game, all featuring an ozone molecule named *Ozzy Ozone*. The third example is the *Map Game* developed by the North Atlantic Treaty Organisation (NATO). The game consists of an interactive map where players have to locate actors and spot information on the twenty-nine NATO members, as well as partnerships with non-NATO countries.

Cases with a regional (i.e. limited to a restricted regional area, as for instance the EU or Eurozone areas) or local (confined to a specific country) outreach are a minority. Take the example of *Pop Hunter*, promoted by the UNDP regional office in China in cooperation with the Chinese Ministry of Environmental Protection. *Pop Hunter* was presented in 2015 as part of an international campaign to raise awareness on Persistent Organic Pollutants (POPs). POPs originate from pesticides, industrial chemicals, and by-products of chemical processes. They accumulate in the body tissues of living organisms and ultimately threaten humans and ecosystems. *Pop Hunter*, available for free download on the Apple Store, challenges players to hunt twenty-three different POPs. Beyond the game, however, the goal is to educate players about the risks of such pollutants. They are encouraged to use the official website of the initiative for additional information, and to participate in online Chinese communities on Weibo (the Chinese equivalent of Twitter) and WeChat. UNESCO's *Sai Fah the Flood Fighter* targets Southeast Asian children.

The UNDP also operates on a smaller scale, at local level. *Youth Work* was designed by the UNDP in partnership with the Ministry of Labour of Bhutan and the US Emerson College to crowdsource creative approaches to tackle the issue of youth unemployment in Bhutan. The game (to be explained later in these pages) solely targeted the Bhutanese community. *Last Exit Flucht* is another case in point. Developed in 2006 by the German representative of the UNHCR, the internet-based game was explicitly designed for teenagers of German-speaking countries. An interesting fact: *Last Exit Flucht* was a reworked version of a similar Swedish-language game, *Mot Alla Odds*, which was designed by UNHCR in Stockholm.

Nothing limits the same supranational regulator from experimenting with gamified governance on different scales at the same time. The EU, for example, implements both global and regional types of gamified policies. *Kids' Corner* exemplifies the former type. Not just EU citizens, but young citizens from non-EU countries are encouraged to learn about the EU project through a number of educational games. Players are challenged with trivia and action games focused on historical, social, legal and political aspects of European integration. Instead, prize competitions target only EU citizens, and thus have a precise regional outreach.

6. World wonders and inflation rates

Moving from the range of supranational gamified governance to the scope, gamified practices may be separated into two main types. Informative gamification pursues an informative goal. Attractive gamification includes those gamified policies designed to engage citizens in participating in supranational policy-making.

This binomial classification is used for understanding the scopes pursued by supranational regulators when introducing new initiatives of gamification; it does not intend to categorise or describe the structure of these initiatives. Irrespective of the typology of gamification used by supranational regulators, in fact, participants of gamified processes held at the supranational level may be required to do something at a particular time or place, or they may enjoy the possibility of affecting the actions of other individuals; alternatively, they may be required to attain a sequence of goals, that are typically ordered at higher levels of complexity and difficulty; they may also be expected to coordinate with other individuals in order to solve a challenge; finally, they may experience a combination of these features. In short, the design and structure of gamified experiments in supranational policy-making complement each other; however, they do not run in tandem, since the structure is generally broader than the aims.

The first type of gamification consists of practices pursuing informative purposes. We have already familiarised ourselves with the link between informative gamification and its global outreach. Let's return to it for a moment. The aim of informative gamification is to raise awareness and spread ideas about topics of interest to supranational regulators through learning processes in which citizens or, as the case may be, their representatives are involved. Hence, the natural association linking informative gamification with global outreach. Cases falling within the former type are designed to provide the largest possible number of players with (direct) knowledge of a given problem as well as (indirect) knowledge of the activity of the supranational regulator who carries the duty to regulate that topic.

In World Wonders, a gamified competition organised by UNESCO, the scope was to inform the public opinion about the importance of the world's cultural heritage, and to acknowledge the role of UNESCO in protecting it. Differently from World Wonders, the Tap Challenge is a case of informative gamification with a local outreach: the American people. We will return to it shortly. Let us first conclude with an example of informative gamified governance operating on a regional level. *Economia* is part of a strategy to inform European citizens, and specifically young generations, about basic principles of economic policy.[8] The strategy includes the *Generation €uro Students' Award* and a cartoon on price stability.

---

[8] The 2016–2020 European e-Government Action Plan promotes efficient and effective digital public services as key components of the EU's Digital Single Market. To achieve this goal, the European Commission indicates a number of actions that public administrations should implement. These include 'the use of opportunities offered by the new digital environment to facilitate interactions with stakeholders'. The underlying principles of the plan include inclusiveness, accessibility, openness and transparency.

The *Generation €uro Students' Award* (another example of prize competition) runs in eleven Eurozone countries each academic year. Students who enter the competition are usually aged between sixteen and nineteen and are in their final years of secondary education. The competition is composed of three rounds. The first consists of an online quiz, the second of an assignment and the third of a presentation followed by a question and answer session. The winning team from each participating country, as well as the winning team from international or European schools, are invited to the ECB in Frankfurt. Here, they take part in a European awards event with the president of the ECB. The cartoon, produced by the ECB in partnership with the national central banks of the Euro area, is aimed at explaining price stability in simple terms, and it is accompanied by a teacher's booklet and a pupil's leaflet.

7. Mobile phones and grains of rice

There are examples of informative gamification in which the educational purpose (players are informed about issues of concern to the supranational regulator that developed the game) is combined with an attempt to raise funds. The *Tap Challenge* sponsored by UNESCO invited Americans to take a break from texting, emailing, tweeting and posting with their mobile phones. For every fifteen minutes spent away from their phones, a pool of donors committed to provide the funding equivalent of one day of clean water for a child.

Another example is *Freerice*, launched in 2009 by the WFP. *Freerice* consists of an online vocabulary game in which donors commit to contributing ten grains of rice to the worlds' poorest for every word a player gets right. Each time players answer a question right, a banner ad seen on the play screen generates enough money for the WFP to buy ten grains of rice to help reach 'Zero Hunger', a UN programme launched in 2012 aimed at eliminating all forms of malnutrition in the world, and at building inclusive and sustainable food systems. Interestingly, the Zero Hunger programme itself includes gamified elements. The programme's website invites participants to sign an online declaration to end malnutrition, download a badge and share it on social media.

8. The 'Evokation'

Attractive gamification includes all gamified processes aimed at fostering citizens' participation. Attractive forms of gamified governance collect ideas from players/participants to be used by supranational regulators in policy-making. The WB's *Evoke* is the main exemplar of this type of gamification. The game was designed to engage a global public in the activities of the WB around the world. Each week a new mission was uploaded to *Evoke*. Players were encouraged to solve the missions by brainstorming together and progressing through three phases: study, action and imagination.[9]

Let us take, by way of example, the first episode of the game. Titled 'Social Innovation', the episode is set in a futuristic Tokyo facing a famine crisis due to the end of rice reserves. After being introduced to the backstory, players were assigned to 'investigate the story'. This phase consisted of finding thirteen secrets, each corresponding to a question. Questions aimed at informing players about key concepts related to the WB's activities, like the following: 'what is food security?' The action phase followed. In this stage players were provided with a preliminary list of websites and biographies of real-life social innovators and were asked to identify their 'hero'. They were also encouraged to friend him/her on Facebook and subscribe to their blog. Finally, players had to document their activities in a blog post. The last phase of the mission challenged players with imagining best-case future scenarios. The ideas had to be formulated in the form of a blog post.

---

[9] See D.I. WADDINGTON, 'A parallel world for the World Bank: A case study of Urgent: Evoke, an educational alternate game', *Revue Internationale des technologies en pédagogie universitaire*, 10, 42-56 (2013).

The same structure was replicated throughout the ten-week cycle of the game. Each mission had a different topic, including sustainable power, empowering women, urban resilience and indigenous networking. Arguably, the whole process was designed to inform citizens about (and engage them with) the WB's activities. Differently from other cases, *Evoke* was also meant to provide the WB with fresh and innovative ideas to be used for future decisions on cooperation for development. In fact, in order to win the game and reclaim the prize (either a scholarship to attend the Evoke Summit in Washington, a mentorship with an experienced social innovator or seed funding worth $1,000) players had to create an 'Evokation' - that is to say, a social innovation project.

9. Regulatory experimentalism

In describing gamification in domestic policies, we introduced three types: informative, attractive and distractive. The distractive type, however, does not appear in supranational gamified policies.

This is a noteworthy observation. At the outset of this chapter, we argued that the remoteness of supranational regulators from citizens' lives and causes has led many in the political and academic arenas to question the legitimate role of supranational regulators. We used this argument to explain why gamification is experimented with more timidity among supranational decision-makers compared with their national counterparts. The same reasoning, we might maintain here, justifies the absence of distractive forms of gamification. Since gamification is used predominantly by supranational regulators to enhance legitimacy there is no need for distractive approaches. Which explains why, if a ranking of experimentalism through regulatory tools (other than hard law) in supranational arenas existed, attractive gamification would probably sit on top.

Let us pick up the experimentalism discourse from where we left off. Supranational regulators, we explained in Chapter 1, are not

4. Gamification Beyond Borders

new to experimenting with policy tools. In order to respond effectively to a changing context of regulatory complexity and uncertainty, supranational regulators have actively promoted innovation in policy-making. The World Trade Organization and the OECD, for instance, have experimented with steering instruments since the 1990s. The WB progressively adapted its policies to the scope of creating valuable outcomes for local communities, rather than on programmed outputs.

The EU is at the forefront of such experiments. In 2011, Simon Hix and Bjorn Hoyland calculated that the EU produces approximately 150 pieces of new legislation each year, more than in most other democratic polities.[10] Over the last decade, however, the annual output of EU directives has sharply declined, replaced by new policy instruments based on cooperation, good practice and voluntary action - the 'experimentalist governance' identified by Sabel and Zeitlin. Typical is the case of the 'open method of coordination', a form of intergovernmental policy-making the common features of which are its legal non-bindingness and its dependence on the will of national governments to comply with it.[11] Experimentalist governance turned out to be useful for dealing with complex and sensitive policy areas.

The relationship between gamification and other tools of governance is not sequential but cumulative. Gamified policies chime well with other types of experiments and their leading principles. To clarify this point, we will keep the focus on EU. Here the introduction of gamified policies has complemented pre-existing forms of governance used to pursue similar scopes (cooperation and deliberation).

---

[10] See S. HIX & B. HOYLAND, *The Political System of the European Union*, Palgrave Macmillan, 2011.

[11] See S. KROGER, 'The end of democracy as we know it? The legitimacy deficits of bureaucratic social policy governance', *European Integration*, 29, 565-582 (2007).

'Orchestration' and 'agile governance' offer valid examples.[12] Orchestrated governance postulates that policy-makers refrain from engaging in regulation in order to facilitate cooperation among multiple intermediaries. The idea behind agile governance is to apply the principles of software development to political settings. These principles include the prevalence of participation over control and dynamic adaptation to changing scenarios. As with the case of gamification, the EU is basically searching for options that could facilitate participation and fast-track solutions to controversies.

10. Blocks and youth workers

How long should an experiment with gamified governance last? The answer depends on the scope and the structure of the experiment. For reasons of simplification, this book distinguishes two main hypotheses: long and short term. The length, as we have said, does not refer to the chronological duration but rather to the repeatability of the same experiment. The proof is that short-term types are in a minority among cases of supranational gamified governance. Most of the cases are long-term. This is probably due to the need for supranational regulators to maximise resources and expected benefits, which is more likely to happen with policies that can be replicated over time.

One good example of a long-term project is *Block by Block*, promoted by UN-Habitat (the UN programme for sustainable cities) since 2012. Each of the UN's *Block by Block* projects starts with drawing up a model of a public space that needs regenerating. To achieve this end UN-Habitat uses Minecraft, the popular video game developed by Mojang. Participants to the projects participate in a workshop where they learn the basics of the game and brainstorm ideas of what they would like the final design to look like.

---

[12] For a brief account of innovative forms of governance, see J.A. HASSELBALCH, 'Innovation assessment: governing through periods of disruptive technological change', *Journal of European Public Policy* (2017).

According to UN-Habitat, more than 17,000 people have been involved in forty-two workshops around the world. Approximately twenty of the fifty *Block by Block* projects run by UN-Habitat have been completed. These include the redesign of Placa Tlaxcoaque in the historic centre of Mexico City, the revitalisation of a former green market located in the municipality of Pristina in Kosovo, and the improvement of sixty public spaces across the city of Nairobi in Kenya.

Regardless of the minor relevance of short-term gamified governance, it is worthwhile expending a few words on it. Let us take the example of UNDP's *Youth Work* to clarify this point. The aim of *Youth Work* was to crowdsource creative approaches to tackle the issue of youth unemployment in Bhutan. The game was officially launched in October 2014. Players could access it online or through SMS. They had to answer questions and complete exercises, progressing through the three missions of the game, each with its own unique theme (e.g. information sources, educational opportunities), in a one-week window. Throughout the process, participants were offered the opportunity to express their opinions about unemployment in Bhutan and deliberate on the best solutions to these problems. Players could also promote and vote on ideas for new projects. The proposals with the most votes were awarded funding at the conclusion of the game. In addition to that, the UNDP and the Bhutanese authorities committed to incorporating the inputs and ideas received by the participants into long-term strategic plans in the country. Something similar happened with *Evoke*. The game was designed to last fourteen weeks—this was, in fact, the timespan that, according to the designers of the game, was considered the most appropriate to maintain a high level of engagement from players, gather a sufficient number of ideas and inform users about the activities of the WB.

5. Gamified Publics

Our journey into gamified governance began with a brief look at its prospects, and questioning its usefulness, durability and desirability. Public regulators, we claimed, face practical and theoretical dilemmas when they introduce badges, points and scoreboards into policy-making. In the previous chapters, we put these dilemmas aside to focus on the descriptive aspects of gamification. This chapter, and that which follows, return to these dilemmas, investigating the promises and exploring the perils of gamified public governance.

Given the complexity of the gamification issue, and the lack of the necessary conceptual models to fully understand the problems that may develop with the increase of gamification in policy-making, this chapter will begin with an attempt to simplify some of the initial concepts; namely, the role and nature of participants in gamified processes. This should be considered as a preliminary attempt to clarify how the publics engaged with gamified policy-making may influence the transformations of current democratic systems.

We have seen that the traditional binomial separation between social groups is no longer viable. As an alternative, we might propose to supplement quantitative assessments of publics with qualitative analysis. Hence, three publics may be attracted by gamified policies—policy-entrepreneurs, citizen-lobbyists and citizen-activists. Although these remain ideal types, the inherent prerogatives of each provide key information to answer the problematic questions related to the gamification of policy-making.

To this end, this chapter makes use of three conceptual lens: prosumerism, collective intelligence and network theory. Once combined, these concepts clarify the nature of the publics and introduce the problems discussed in Chapter 6.

1. Hard-core participants vs. unqualified masses

The Brazilian philosopher Umberto Unger has argued that in contemporary democracies it is crucial to enable people to see themselves as individuals capable of escaping their confined roles.[1] Let us take it from here. The idea of citizens playing 'roles' in democracies brings us to our first dilemma: what kind of citizenship is nurtured by gamified policy-making?

There are two approaches to answer this question. The first builds on the distinction between 'hard-core participants' and 'unqualified masses'.[2] Plenty of studies on participation make use of this categorisation. Hard-core participants are people who participate a lot. Thanks to their commitment, they become extraordinary experts on specific issues and dominate participation. They are, however, a minority. Only those citizens with preferential access to three fundamental resources - time, money and knowledge - can be included in this category. The hard-core participant's identikit is easy to sketch: male, college-educated, middle-aged and wealthier than the average citizen.

Unqualified masses are on the opposite end of the spectrum. This is a large social group. It includes citizens who participate occasionally, who generally do not commit for long periods, and show little interest in engaging in conventional forms of participation. Unqualified masses include women, racial and linguistic minorities, and people with low-paid jobs and poor education.

The differential of power between these two types of citizens has

---

[1] See R. UNGER, *Democracy Realized: The Progressive Alternative*, Verso, 1998.
[2] See, for instance, LERNER, *Making Democracy Fun*.

three implications. The first concerns civic participation and technology. Scholars have used the differential of power between citizens to explain why participation is (and remains) fundamentally unequal. Arend Lijphart described it as 'the unresolved dilemma of democracy'; a dilemma that - according to many - the diffusion of technologies in the public sector has left unresolved, or even accrued.[3]

On this point, reinforcement theorists emphasise the strong tie between socio-economic status and online political and civic engagement.[4] Pippa Norris, for example, suggests that those who are already engaged in offline avenues are more willing to engage online; however, she adds, those lacking in knowledge and interests in political and civic activities will be no more likely to engage in online forms of participation.[5]

In disagreement with such sceptical viewpoints are those scholars - among them the mobilisation theorists - who are optimistic about the potential for the internet to increase the quality of democratic governance. Halfway between sceptics and optimists we find scholars like Archon Fung and Hollie Russon Gilman. They identify six models of how digital technologies might affect democratic politics: the empowered public sphere, displacement of traditional organisations by new digitally self-organised groups, digitally direct democracy, truth-based advocacy, constituent mobilisation, and crowdsourced social monitoring. Compared to their reinforcement theorist colleagues, Fung and Russon Gilman regard with optimism the potential of the internet to level differentials of power. Yet, in three of their

---

[3] See A. LIJPHART, 'Unequal participation: democracy's unresolved dilemma', *American Political Science Review*, 91, 1-14 (1997).
[4] See, among others, A. SMITH, K.L. SCHLOZMAN, S. VERBA & H.E. BRADY, *The Internet and Civic Engagement*, Pew Internet & American Life Project, 2009.
[5] See P. NORRIS, 'Preaching to the converted? Pluralism, participation and party websites', *Party Politics*, 9, 21-45 (2003). Some disagree, accusing reinforcement theorists of falling into the epistemic trap of technological determinism. See G. AICHHOLZER & D. ALLHUTTER, *Online Forms of Political Participation and their Impact on Democracy*, Austrian Academy of Sciences, 2009.

models they acknowledge the existence of biases that might counterweight the incremental contributions of technology to democracy.[6]

Moving to the second implication. The differential of power among social groups can also be used to interpret the crisis of democracy. Every time a new study focusing on the real impact of participatory democracy is published, the results are, at best, discouraging. Martin Gilens demonstrated that the opinions of the bottom 90% of income earners in America have a 'minuscule, near-zero, statistically non-significant impact' on politics.[7]

The same conclusions have been reached by scholars who have analysed the scarce impact of the large majority of the population on their political systems.[8] A few analysts even go so far as to maintain that democracies should be replaced with different (i.e. more efficient) systems of government, like David Van Reybrouck and Jason Brennan. The former suggests appointing representatives on the basis of chance; the latter proposes to shift from democracy to 'epistocracies'.[9] Van Reybrouck considers elections the 'fossil fuel of politics'. He suggests replacing them with more efficient and less expensive randomly-selected juries. Brennan's argument is clear: we should hope for less, not more, participation. Most people should not worry at all about politics, leaving public engagement to a small number of individuals. After all, advocates of the necessity of attributing governmental responsibilities to educated elites rather than common citizens include Freud, Aristotle and Plato, who he described ordinary men, in contrast to philosophers, as unable to make judgments about the common good in *The Republic*.

Third, and last consequence: the differential of power is used to criticise attempts to reform democratic systems. Theda Skocpol, to

---

[6] See FUNG ET AL. 'Six models', 30.
[7] See M. GILENS & B.I. PAGE, 'Testing theories of American politics: elites, interest groups, and average citizens', *Perspectives on Politics*, 12, 564-581 (2014).
[8] See, for instance, T. FERGUSON, *Golden Rule: The Investment Theory of Party Competition and the Logic of Money-Driven Political Systems*, University of Chicago Press, 1995.
[9] See D. VAN REYBROUCK, *Against Elections: The Case for Democracy*, Penguin, 2013; J. BRENNAN, *Against Democracy*, Princeton University Press, 2016.

name but one, criticises political plans that suggest revitalising democracies through enhancing digital tools, exactly because these studies ignore more profound issues of economic inequality and power disparity.[10]

2. Breaking free from quantitative assessments

There is a second, more elaborated, approach to understanding what types of citizens are nurtured by gamified policies. This approach moves from logical and empirical premises. The logical premise considers the sole quantitative criterion unrealistic to assess the willingness of citizens to participate. Confronted with a barrage of media (and, more recently, of scholarly) essays on the issue, it is easy to forget that gamification still generates a minute portion of participation in governance.

A qualitative dimension, the logical argument goes, is also necessary. The empirical premise confirms this assumption. We know that several participatory platforms (both online and offline) are explicitly designed to trigger a response only when the number of participants reaches a pre-set benchmark. The higher the number of signatories of online petitioning initiatives, the more likely governments are to respond.[11] The criteria to define how many participants is 'enough', however, are subjective, and thus impossible to define a priori.

A few examples may help to clarify this point. Let us take the case of *Evoke*. Only 223 players completed the game. Of these, just seventy were certified as a 'World Bank Institute Social Innovator'. Even lower was the number of players who submitted an 'Evokation proposal'. However, the total number of active users throughout the duration of the game, according to the WB, exceeded 4,600 people.

---

[10] See T. SKOCPOL, *Diminished Democracy: From Membership to Management in American Civic Life*, University of Oklahoma Press, 2003.
[11] See T. PEIXOTO & J. FOX, *When Does ICT-Enabled Citizen Voice Lead to Government Responsiveness?* World Development Report, 2016.

Let's look at another case. The first version of *Youth Work* gathered only 2,000 participants. For this reason, the following year (2015) the UNDP decided to improve the participation rate by lowering the barrier to access the game, through the creation of a table top game that would enable small group discussions within safe, non-judgmental environments. The number of participants consequently multiplied.

The Russian app *Active Citizen* is a third case in point. Of the approximately eleven million residents of Moscow, two million have participated in the polls administered through the platform since 2014. Not much, quantitatively speaking. But we know that the majority of participants are enthusiastic about the service and that the number of new participants is rising.

Fourth, and finally, we have the example of *Decide Madrid*. The two ideas that in 2017 passed the 1% threshold set by the platform, collected approximately 27,000 votes each (Madrid has 2.7 million eligible voters). Shall we consider this an appropriate threshold? Interviewed on this topic, Miguel Arana, director of the Proyecto de Participación del Ayuntamiento de Madrid, explains why the 1% threshold is low only in appearance. Those who support a proposal are citizens who have shown a strong commitment throughout a long process: from registering, to reading proposals, up to supporting those they consider relevant, and informing other people about them.[12]

What do these examples tell us? That breaking free from quantitative assessment is beneficial in three ways. First, it opens up to accepting, and classifying, sporadic participation as meaningful participation. Alongside citizens who have the resources (and the motivation) to impact on policy-making, and beside those who neglect participating, there are citizens who activate only when they perceive a threat to their personal interests.

---

[12] See M. DESERIIS, 'Limits to the scalability of online participation in the 15-M and Podemos: An interview with Miguel Arana', *Scalable Democracy*, 14 January 2018, available at https://scalingdemocracy.net.

Second, it provides added value to the distinction between conventional and unconventional forms of participation. In Chapter 1, we reported the academic voices that argue that rising forms of non-conventional participation have replaced declining forms of conventional engagement. Stephen Coleman's autonomous citizens, or the quiet citizens described by the Woolf Institute are good examples of unconventional forms of civic engagement. Using the binary distinction of hard-core participants/unqualified masses would lead us to describe autonomous and quiet citizens as unqualified masses. We know instead that these citizens engage in unconventional forms of participation, which in turn supports the assumption that they could be attracted by gamified forms of governance.

Third, and subsequently, escaping quantitative accounts paves the way to accepting that democratic systems are composed of multiple types of publics. In this respect, this book agrees with Nancy Fraser's claim, in that it recognises, and favours, a 'multiplicity of publics' over a 'single public'. 'Subaltern counter-publics', as Nancy Fraser named them, are important too. These include minor voices that coalesce around common issues, circulate counter-discourses and formulate oppositional interpretations of issues.[13]

3. Constituting the demos

So how to practically move from the traditional, outdated, distinction of participatory publics to a new one that better describes the civic interests attracted by gamified policy-making? This book identifies three main typologies of participants in the framework of gamified governance. The first type is 'policy-entrepreneurs', that is, self-conscious citizens who choose to participate because they share an interest in tailoring public policies for their and common interests. The second type is 'citizen-lobbyists' and includes all citizens who

---

[13] See N. FRASER, 'Rethinking the public sphere: A contribution to the critique of actually existing democracy', *Social Text*, 25/26, 56-80 (1990).

use gamified mechanisms to leverage policy-making in their favour. The third type is 'citizen-activists' who are socially engaged citizens advocating towards public decision-makers.

Before proceeding with a description of these three typologies, however, two brief notes are required. First, this categorisation is by no means exclusive or fully comprehensive. In fact, the three types of public can complement each other. Policy-entrepreneurs, for example, can be seen as a more professionalised version of citizen-lobbyists; and, to some extent, citizen-activists can be considered as citizen-lobbyists with a values-oriented approach.

Second, and most importantly, we should keep in mind that the concept of public might vary a great deal if we consider participatory processes at the national or supranational levels. 'Constituting the demos', as Robert Goodin names it, is already a problem discussed among democratic theorists at the national level.[14] In the supranational arena this becomes an even greater issue. Environmental, economic, social and political problems expand beyond national borders, and generate patterns of interests that, in the view of many observers, impact on the size and shape of constituencies. Some studies divide the public in two broad categories: 'attentive' and 'committed'.

The former category includes the portion of the broader general public that shares the same issue-perspectives and values. Attentive publics are based on solidarity. They are open to anyone who shares the values or issue position that they advocate for. Philip Lowe and Jane Goyder make the case with environmentalists. To be considered environmentalist, they explain, one does not need to be a member of any environmental advocacy group.[15] Committed publics, by contrast, formally commit to objectives and values, usually via provision of membership fees or donations.

---

[14] See R.E. GOODIN, 'Enfranchising all affected interests, and its alternatives', *Philosophy and Public Affairs*, 35, 40-68 (2007).
[15] See P. LOWE & J GOYDER, *Environmental Groups in Politics*, George Allen & Unwin, 1983.

4. Ties and engagements

Attentive groups populate supranational arenas. Some scholars prefer using the definition of 'distributed public' to describe the characteristics of the public that is engaged in transnational democracy.[16]

Beyond terminology, distributed and attentive publics share the same features. It is posited that, in the supranational arena, the distributed public replaces traditional democratic intermediaries. It is unlikely, however, that the distributed (or attentive) public could be transformed into a convergent strong public (in other words, a committed public) whose decisions constitute a single normative will. To do so would require a public at the same global scale; but this public would face three strong limitations: financial, linguistic and interactive.

Financially speaking, to engage citizens across different geographical locations may be expensive. Offline variants imply travel and subsistence costs. Online variants may be cheaper, but certainly are not cost-free. At a minimum they involve technical and facilitation costs. Second, a global public faces linguistic limitations. Citizens who are not competent in the requisite language (usually English) are marginalised. We will return to this issue in the next chapter. Finally, but most importantly, there is an 'interactive' limitation. Citizens that engage on a transnational level often lack the interactive dimension of mutual claims.

In a famous essay the economist William Nordhaus once noted that there is 'no mechanism by which global citizens can make binding collective decisions'.[17] We can hardly argue against that. Representational logics demand the capacity to engage directly with other stakeholders, often face to face. Transnational ties, instead, are

---

[16] See J. BOHMAN, *Democracy across Borders: From Dêmos to Dêmoi*, MIT Press, 2007.
[17] See W.D. NORDHAUS, *Paul Samuelson and Global Public Goods: A commemorative essay for Paul Samuelson*, in M. SZENBERG, L. RAMRATTAN & A.A. GOTTESMAN (eds.), *Samuelsonian Economics and the Twenty-First Century*, 88-98, Oxford University Press, 2006.

'weak' by definition. These ties are formed by tiny acts of participation, like sharing tests or images related to a political issue or signing up to a digital campaign (about which we will discuss more when analysing network theory).

Some venture to say that transnational participation translates into 'thin' engagement (faster, easier and potentially viral - it encompasses mainly online activities that allow people to express opinions and affiliate themselves with a particular cause) as opposed to 'thick' engagement (intensive, informed and deliberative - it relies on small-group settings, either online or offline, in which people decide how they want to help to solve problems), which is distinctive of national participatory experiences.[18]

As a way to escape these puzzling limitations, Jacqueline Best and Alexandra Gheciu go even further than the idea of the distributed public and suggest that, in contemporary global governance, we should transcend the view of the public as a separate or distinct entity or social space. Rather, they suggest, we should see the public as a 'practice', that is, as meaningful patterns of activity that enables individuals and communities to reproduce in the world. Hence the conclusion of Best and Gheciu: by reconceptualising the public as a practice forces us to examine how different kinds of actors and activities get counted as public in different contexts.[19]

Regardless of the validity of Best and Gheciu's theory, the following pages will have to take into account the difference between the concept of public at the national and supranational levels. Unless otherwise specified, the description of publics will refer to domestic experiments of gamified policy-making. For the same reason, the following table (TABLE 3) shows which public was involved in national gamified policies.

---

[18] See, for instance, INSTITUTE OF DEVELOPMENT STUDIES, *Transforming Governance: What Role for Technologies?* 2016, available at https://opendocs.ids.ac.uk.
[19] See J. BEST & A. GHECIU (eds.), *The Return of the Public in Global Governance*, Cambridge University Press, 2014.

Table 3. Publics in national gamified policy-making

CASE	PUBLICS		
	Policy Entrepreneurs	Citizen Lobbyists	Citizen Activists
Run That Town	X		
B3—Design your Marketplace!		X	X
MMOGWLI	X		
The Red Balloon Challenge	X	X	
CitySwipe	X	X	X
Smart Pune	X		
Manor Labs	X	X	X
Macon Money			
Decide Madrid	X	X	X
Decidim	X	X	X
Gallinazo Avisa			X

5. Gamified publics no. 1 - policy-entrepreneurs

The first ideal type of citizen attracted by gamified governance is the policy-entrepreneur. There is a vast academic literature aimed at describing policy-entrepreneurs. John Kingdon was one of the first scholars, in 1984, to use this expression. He named policy-entrepreneurs those actors who use their knowledge of political processes to further their own policy ends. These may be elected politicians or leaders of interest groups who seek to exploit windows of opportunity to promote their solutions to policy-makers.[20]

Similar to Kingdon, in 1999 Peter John focused his description of policy-entrepreneurs on their ability to try out a combination of

---

[20] See J.W. KINGDON, *Agendas, Alternatives, and Public Policies*, Little, Brown & Co., 1984.

ideas to influence policy-making.[21] More recently, Mark Zupan described the vulnerability of governments to 'government insiders'. These can be found in both autocratic and democratic political systems and have the motive and means to co-opt political power in their benefit and at the expense of national well-being.[22]

In describing a policy-entrepreneur, this book moves away from these negative connotations, as well as from those descriptions of policy-entrepreneurs as civil servants that bring new policy ideas into the open and promote policy change.[23] In the context of gamified public governance, policy-entrepreneurs are seen as highly skilled citizens capable of mobilising expertise, intervening in gamified processes, and eventually benefiting from them. A definition that combines policy transfer theory - where entrepreneurs are civic actors who promote best practices across legal systems - with rational choice theory, where 'entrepreneur' is used to define individuals who seek to provide public services or form interest groups (indirectly benefiting from it).

Let us stop for a second. As banal as it may seem, there is a question we should answer before proceeding: are policy-entrepreneurs real? According to many academics the answer is no, not really, or not necessarily. It is a common assumption of many papers discussing participatory initiatives that participants are - or should be - non-experts. Professionalisation, goes on this assumption, is at odds with participation. Amateurs, rather than skilled and professionalised individuals, should opt in and populate participatory processes.

If you think about it, the word 'crowd' is reminiscent of citizens who, from a large group of people, self-select to participate. In theory, this includes the entire pool of people who have access to the

---

[21] See P. JOHN, 'Is there life after policy streams, advocacy coalitions, and punctuations: using evolutionary theory to explain policy change?', *Policy Studies Journal*, 31.4, 481-498 (2003).
[22] See M.A. ZUPAN, *Inside Job: How Government Insiders Subvert the Public Interest*, Cambridge University Press, 2017.
[23] See, for instance, T. KALIL, 'Policy entrepreneurship at the White House: Getting things done in large organizations', *Innovations*, 11, 4-21 (2017).

internet and are aware of the task and the possibility of participating. In theory, but not in reality. The notion of a crowd of amateurs is a false assumption - or a myth to debunk, as Brabham suggests.[24] Empirical research on crowdsourcing initiatives submits something different from what we just reported: that publics opting into crowdsourcing arrangements are frequently self-selected professionals and experts.

Our question has been answered. Policy-entrepreneurs are sufficiently numerous to be defined as a self-standing group in the context of participatory processes and their contribution is weighted as increasingly important by regulators aimed at cooperating with civic actors through gamified policies.

In this regard, the research of Satish and Prya Nambisan on co-creation of public services is particularly interesting.[25] They maintain that any government or public body interested in engaging citizens in the construction of public services, should neglect the quantity of inputs provided by participants, and should focus on the quality of the contribution that each participant can provide. According to Nambisans, citizens who contribute to civic problem-solving may assume four different roles. The first role is the 'citizen-explorer'—that is, citizens who are active in discovering, identifying, defining and circulating civic problems that need to be solved. Typically, citizens-explorers are those engaged in using apps like *Street Bump*, *FixMyStreet* or *PorMiBarrio* where users are encouraged to detect issues in the neighbourhood streets.

The second role is the 'citizen-ideator'. Citizen-ideators are those capable of envisioning solutions to civic problems. Usually these citizens come up with innovative ideas to solve problems that are already known. The public challenges launched by the US govern-

---

[24] See D.C. BRABHAM, 'The myth of amateur crowds: A critical discourse analysis of crowdsourcing coverage', *Information, Communication & Society*, 15, 394-410 (2012).
[25] See S. NAMBISAN & P. NAMBISAN, *Engaging Citizens in Co-Creation in Public Services: Lessons Learned and Best Practices*, IBM Center for the Business of Government, 2013.

ment and the EU Commission, and more generally all crowdsourcing initiatives driven by public regulators, are based on this idea: to offer users the opportunity to suggest innovative ideas. To provide an illustration of this approach we can look at the *Tag Challenge* (described in Chapter 3). The challenge was awarded to Crowdscanner, a team composed of computer scientists from American and British universities.

So why do policy-entrepreneurs, described as ideators, find gamified public challenges attractive? For three reasons. First, participating in such challenges is demanding in terms of expertise and skills (that policy-entrepreneurs might be able to provide); second, participants in challenges bear costs (both in terms of participating fees and time) that the majority of ordinary citizens are unable to cover; third, gamified challenges attract participants who have personal interests at stake—for example, the need to be visible in the relevant market or the necessity to get credited. When the Indian Government launched the *Smart Pune* app, a gamified public challenge aimed at providing support for the municipality of Pune, 40,000 innovators presented solutions for ameliorating the lives of citizens. They were motivated by the opportunity to enhance their credibility and benefit their businesses.

Finally, the third and fourth categories of citizens identified by the Nambisans are 'citizen-designers' (those capable of designing solutions to civic problems) and the 'citizen-diffusers' (those who support and diffuse public services innovations among the population).

6. Gamified publics no. 2 – citizen-lobbyists

The term citizen-lobbyist returned to fashion recently. In his most recent book, Alberto Alemanno optimistically depicts citizen-lobbyists as the present and future of civic engagement.[26] Alemanno

---

[26] See A. ALEMANNO, *Lobbying for Change: Find Your Voice to Create a Better Society*, Icon, 2017.

moves from the same crucial assumption made at the outset of this book—that civil society is experiencing a crisis of faith, feeling increasingly disconnected from governing institutions. In spite of what populist movements argue, referenda and direct democracy have not provided citizens with the right tools to shape and change policies. After all, he continues, civil society groups can no longer compete (if they ever could) with corporate counterparts. Alemanno sketches a process to transform citizens into lobbyists, capable of advancing causes they care about, from saving a local library to tacking action against fracking.

Amanda Knief depicts citizen-lobbyists in a similar fashion. She also moves from the assumption that more citizen involvement is needed in governmental processes; she thus explains how citizens could become more engaged grassroots activists and influence policy-making.[27] Many other authors follow the same path. Manuel Arriaga's pamphlet argues for five measures to 'reboot democracies', all of which revolving around common citizens.[28]

This book does not engage directly with theories promoting the role of actively engaged citizens who represent their interests, as if they were operating as professional lobbyists. Rather, it borrows this definition because it perfectly describes those citizens who envisage in gamified governance a channel to leverage policy-making in their favour.

Are citizens-lobbyists comparable to policy-entrepreneurs? Yes and no. Both share the same drive: to gain benefits from engaging in gamified governance. After all, the sample used in this book shows that in five out of the six cases of national gamified governance in which citizen-lobbyists were involved, policy-entrepreneurs were also engaged (see TABLE 3). The relationship that policy-entrepreneurs and citizen-lobbyists have with regulators through gamified

---

[27] See A. KNIEF, *The Citizen Lobbyist: A How-To Manual for Making Your Voice Heard in the Government*, Pitchstone, 2013.
[28] See M. ARRIAGA, *Rebooting Democracy: A Citizen's Guide to Reinventing Politics*, Thistle Publishing, 2014.

governance is reminiscent of the Crusoe–Friday model used by James Buchanan and Gordon Tullock in their famous book *The Calculus of Consent*.[29] Crusoe is the better fisherman, while Friday is better at climbing coconut palms. They enter into exchange because they find it mutually advantageous. All things being equal, policy-entrepreneurs, citizen-lobbyists and public regulators find it mutually advantageous to enter into political exchange and to devote resources to a common good: a more participated decision-making.

Yet citizen-lobbyists, differently from policy-entrepreneurs, have a direct and personal interest in becoming directly engaged in policy-making. For this reason, they are similar to Joel Penney's 'citizen-marketers'.[30] The citizen-marketer, explains Penney, is guided by the logics of marketing practice. He/she actively circulates persuasive media to further political interests (including the using protest symbols in social media profile pictures, strategically tweeting links to news articles to raise awareness about select issues or displaying mass-produced T-shirts, buttons, and bumper stickers that promote a favoured electoral candidate or cause). Penney's citizen-marketers view participation in political activities not with regards to producing a collective benefit, but also in how it may shape or influence the outcomes, and as a statement of their own identity.

7. Capturing the regulators

Having clarified the difference between policy-entrepreneurs and citizen-lobbyists, another question arises. Should we apply the public choice theory of 'capture of the regulator' to citizen-lobbyists?[31] Both negative and positive responses have practical consequences.

Answering in the affirmative could lead to the view that to avoid

---

[29] See J.M. BUCHANAN & G. TULLOCK, *The Calculus of Consent: Logical Foundations of Constitutional Democracy*, Liberty Fund, 1962.
[30] See J. PENNEY, *The Citizen Marketer: Promoting Political Opinion in the Social Media Age*, Oxford University Press, 2017.
[31] See G. STIGLER, 'The theory of economic regulation', *The Bell Journal of Economic Regulation and Science*, 2, 3-21(1971).

the risk of capture, public regulators should refrain from (or limit) using gamification practices too intensely; or that, alternatively, regulators should limit themselves to experimenting with distractive forms of gamification. Only experts who possess sound information should take public decisions, claimed Walter Lippmann, in order to safeguard the quality of decisions. The decisions taken on the basis of public debate, he explained, could be easily manipulated by elites.[32]

The opposite, however, is also true. Gamification may be used to respond to what David Easton termed 'authoritative allocations of values', meaning the formulation and implementation of policies that are closely associated with those who hold positions of authority in a political system (and that, consequently, set the goals towards which that system may be directed).[33] Cass Sunstein uses the definition of 'behavioural bureaucrats' to describe the same phenomenon. These are public officials who not only are adversely affected by the standard behavioural biases, but also subjected to the pressure imposed by well-organised private groups with a significant stake in the outcome.[34]

In reality, this book argues that it is unlikely that citizen-lobbyists may end up capturing the regulator. It suffices to observe offline participatory practices. With very few exceptions, business interests are predominant compared to civil society interests. On average, out of every 100 organisations that spend the most on lobbying in developed countries, ninety-five represent business.[35] In the EU, non-profit organisation Lobbyfacts reports that business accounts for roughly 90% of all reported lobbying expenditure. As a result, according to Transparency International, 75% of declared lobbying meetings between lobbyists and public authorities in the first half of

---

[32] See W. LIPPMANN, *Public Opinion*, Harcourt, Brace, & Co., 1921.
[33] See D. EASTON, *A Systems Analysis of Political Life*, John Wiley, 1965.
[34] See T. KURAN & C.S. SUNSTEIN, 'Availability cascades and risk regulation', *Stanford Law Review*, 51, 683-691 (1999).
[35] See L. DRUTMAN, *The Business of America is Lobbying: How Corporations Became Politicized and Politics Became More Corporate*, Oxford University Press, 2015.

2015 were with corporate companies or consultancy firms. Only 18% were with CSOs.[36]

In the US, the non-profit Center for Responsive Politics calculated that the $2.6 billion reportedly spent on lobbying by the corporate sector in 2015 adds up to more than the combined budgets of the Senate ($860 million) and the House of Representatives ($1.18 billion). We may recall Change.gov, the web platform that Barack Obama's team made available to American citizens in the days leading up to his inauguration as president. The results of Change.gov were far from Obama's team expected. Seven of the top ten issues of the platform were about the exact same thing: legalising marijuana in order to tax it and create jobs from this new industry. It turned out later that the design of Change.org privileged small groups of coordinated actors versus larger, diffuse groups of citizens.

For the sake of clarity: the risk of regulatory capture is not exclusive of organised interests. On the contrary, common citizens can also be agents of capture. In the case of the *Speed Camera Lottery* (analysed in Chapter 3), the municipality of Stockholm had to suspend the lottery when it discovered that some drivers had started circling around the cameras to increase their likelihood of winning a prize.

8. Gamified publics no. 3 - citizen-activists

Admittedly, even if the number of policy-entrepreneurs and citizen-lobbyists were combined, it would only account for a narrow slice of the citizenry in Western democracies. The quality, quantity and scopes of their engagement in policy-making may certainly differ, yet both policy-entrepreneurs and citizen-lobbyists share a mature knowledge and appreciation of the benefits that might arise from their direct participation in public decision-making. This is, however, a condition that clashes with the original assumption of this

---

[36]See TRANSPARENCY INTERNATIONAL, *Lobby Meetings with EU Policy-Makers Dominated by Corporate Interests*, 2015.

book. Once we accept that, given the overspread of political disaffection and civic disengagement, the majority of citizens do not fall within either of these categories, we can conclude that public regulators have easy game in engaging them, with or without the use of gamified strategies.

Don Elliott, former general counsel of the EPA, once compared notice and comment to Kabuki theatre: 'a highly stylized process for displaying in a formal way the essence of something which in real life takes place in other venues'.[37] Also Cass Sunstein, borrowing the term made famous by Albert Hirschman,[38] admits that nudging may be 'futile', meaning that the consequences of choice architecture on citizens' choices might have little or no impact at all. This might happen, for instance, when the chooser has already a strongly defined preference that happens to be contrary to that promoted by the regulator. An alternative hypothesis is that futility may even be an intentional outcome for the public regulator. Strategies of gamification, in other words, could be undertaken by public regulators as a way to preserve their decisional autonomy and minimise the possibility of having their decisions reversed or opposed.

Before accepting the validity of this conclusion, however, one should consider the last type of citizens that are attracted by gamified governance—citizen-activists. Who are the citizen-activists? The term 'citizenization' captures the core meaning of this definition. Citizenization was coined by the American activist Pedja Stojicic, who uses it to describe an intentional process of creating the conditions for professionals (and other community members) to 'flex their civic muscle', as for instance developing and practicing social responsibility and becoming active agents in system transformation.[39] To exemplify citizenization, Stojicic uses the example of health professionals: whether they could intentionally use 10% of their time

---

[37] See E.D. ELLIOTT, 'Re-inventing rulemaking', *Duke Law Journal*, 41, 1490-1496 (1992).
[38] See A. HIRSCHMAN, *The Rhetoric of Reaction*, Harvard University Press, 1991.
[39] See P. STOJICIC, 'Let's help health professionals build their civic muscle', 9 June 2017, *The ReThinker's Blog*, available at www.rethinkhealth.org.

to create a culture of health in the interests of community health. Citizen-activists do not envisage nor they seek benefits from participating in policy-making—a situation that separates them from citizen-entrepreneurs and citizen-lobbyists. Citizen-activists 'engage' themselves in participation when they perceive that their voice may produce social impact.

Walter Lippmann argued something very similar over a century ago.[40] Lippmann's claim is that the notion of 'public' as an entity with demarcated interests is futile. It is exactly the opposite, he argues. The public can be described as a dynamic entity that coalesces around certain issues when they believe that for some reason, that issue needs to be advocated for. Issues and publics are linked in a cyclical pattern; the former create the latter as much as the latter generate the former.

A glance across news headlines from the past few years sheds light on this concept. A series of protests were all motivated by the desire to counteract decisions that were going to affect their sphere of values, whether it was the environment, civil rights, gender equality, security or transparency. Take 2017, for example, which witnessed a protest against the ban on abortion in Poland, popular demand in Romania urging the government to reverse a decision of a corruption investigation against officials, and widespread protests in Budapest against Prime Minister Viktor Orban's attacks on civil society institutions. It also saw mass gun control movements initiated by teenagers in the US and, at the global level, the massive and ongoing protest against sexual harassment, pivoted around the #MeToo movement.

Now that we have established the existence of a broad public (or, at least, broader than the two traditionally defined) that may be attracted by gamified governance, we should no longer ask whether citizens can be engaged as such, but rather if gamification can replicate the positive results achieved elsewhere, for instance in climate

---

[40] See W. LIPPMANN, *The Phantom Public*, Harcourt, Brace, & Co., 1925.

change activism. Chapter 2 showed how gamified activism on climate change has attracted wide audiences and helped to overcome some of the obstacles that hinder popular support for civic action.[41] The sample used in this book shows that citizen-activists were mobilised in several cases. Not accidentally, all these cases involved controversial aspects, such as the allocation of city budgeting, urban planning or environmental issues.

9. Gamified publics and governance no. 1 - prosumerism

How does the public(s) engagement with gamified policy-making influence the transformations of current democratic governance? Three conceptual lenses will help us answer this question: prosumerism, collective intelligence and network theory.

Coined in 1980, prosumerism describes a market in which the basic needs of consumers are already satisfied by mass production and companies initiate processes of mass personalisation through mass-producing highly personalised products.[42] Prosumers participate both in the design (as producers) and in the consumption (as consumers) of products through mass customisation. All things being equal, prosumers of public policies contribute to the 'creation' of policies, the same policies that will affect their individual spheres. Co-creation develops through the active flow and exchange of ideas and information between and across citizens and public administrators. This flow facilitates both engagement and empowerment of civic actors in all stages of policy-making.

Take the case of *Run That Town*. The immediate aim of the game was to create awareness among Australian citizens of the role of the census in shaping the direction of policy and its impacts on daily life. In the long run, however, the Australian Census Bureau aimed at producing a positive impact on the engagement of citizens in the

---

[41] In the field of climate change activism the most recurrent issues are eco-detachment and the perception of environmental sustainability as complex and boring.
[42] See A. TOFFLER, *The Third Wave*, Bantam Books, 1984.

decisions concerning the Australian population at large. As reported by the chief creative officer of the company that developed the app: 'we're not just telling people about the data – we're giving them a chance to use it for themselves. It's an innovative way to make those numbers really mean something to the people using them, and to get the community more involved in Census data'.[43]

10. Gamified publics and governance no. 2 – collective intelligence

At the outset of this book, gamification in public governance was compared to crowdsourcing: both combine a bottom-up, open, creative process with top-down organisational goals. An alternative way to answer the question concerning the impact that the public(s) engaged by gamified governance may have on democratic governance is through the lens of collective intelligence—a concept that is strictly related with crowdsourcing.[44] Public institutions that experiment in crowdsourcing, in fact, rely on the collective intelligence of experiment participants.

Collective intelligence, explains Geoff Mulgan, may be understood according to three quantitative variants. The narrow variant is concerned with modalities of online cooperation of groups of people. This reflects the research of Joseph Licklider, who pioneered the study of artificial intelligence. Licklider claimed that the most effective intelligences will not replace human with machine capability. Rather, they will couple humans and digital networks. On the other side of the spectrum, collective intelligence can be used to encompass the whole of human civilisation and culture. Mid-variants include forms of intelligence occurring on a large scale.

---

[43] Interview is available at www.campaignbrief.com/2013/05/the-australian-bureau-of-stati.html.
[44] On collective intelligence, see J.B. SMITH, *Collective Intelligence in Computer-Based Collaboration*, Laurence Erlbaum Associates, 1994; C.R. SUNSTEIN, *Infotopia: How Many Minds Produce Knowledge*, Oxford University Press, 2006.

5. Gamified Publics

Some describe this latter variant as the 'wisdom of the crowd'. This, explains James Surowiecki, is the type of wisdom that originates from the aggregation of a crowd's preferences.[45] Large groups of contributors that are appropriately independent, motivated and informed can collectively make better judgments than the individuals that make them up. Actually, the larger is the crowd, the better the chances of finding the correct solution to a problem. In 2010, a team of researchers in Zurich estimated that if a million individuals were to contribute towards answering a problem via crowdsourcing, they would have a 97.7% likelihood of solving it correctly.[46] The phenomenon was first observed in 1907 by Sir Francis Galton. Galton described a carnival game in which participants could guess the weight of an ox. As people made their estimates, Galton recorded them and observed that the median - which at the time he described as *Vox Populi* - was remarkably close to the correct answer.[47]

A number of empirical studies have assessed the idea of collective intelligence (or wisdom of the crowd) in deliberative processes. John Dryzek, for instance, writes of 'citizen competence' in his studies on citizen deliberation.[48] James Fishkin describes individuals composing citizens' panels as 'better informed and good at taking decisions'.[49] Similar conclusions are drawn by research conducted by

---

[45] See J. SUROWIECKI, *The Wisdom of Crowds*, Doubleday 2004.
[46] See T. BUECHELER, J.H. SIEG, R.M. FUECHSLIN & R. PFEIFER, 'Crowdsourcing, open innovation and collective intelligence in the scientific method: A research agenda and operational framework' in H. FELLERMANN ET AL. (eds.), *Artificial Life XII: Proceedings of the Twelfth International Conference on the Synthesis and Simulation of Living Systems*, MIT Press, 2010.
[47] See F. GALTON, 'The ballot-box', *Nature*, 75 (1952). Over the years scholars have attempted to find the wisdom of the crowd through scaling up or scaling down group interactions in deliberative processes. See, for instance, A. GOEL & D.T. LEE, *Large-scale Deliberation via Small Group Interactions, and the Importance of Triads*, University of Stanford Research Paper, 2010.
[48] See J.S. DRYZEK, A. BACHTIGER & K. MILEWICZ, 'Toward a deliberative global citizens' assembly', *Global Policy*, 2 (2011).
[49] See J.S. FISHKIN, *When the People Speak: Deliberative Democracy and Public Consultation*, Oxford University Press, 2011.

John Gastil.[50] Another author, Pierre Lévy, describes collective intelligence as an alternative source of power.[51] Collective intelligence, according to Lévy, allows grassroots communities to respond effectively to public powers. In collective intelligence, explains Lévy, everyone knows something and nobody knows everything, thus it is the group as a whole that can tap into what any one person knows.

Clickworkers is an interesting case of practical application of the wisdom of the crowd from a public institution. Initiated in the year 2000 as a pilot study by NASA to determine whether or not online volunteers would be interested in contributing, and if they could produce data useful to answering interesting science questions, it asked users to identify craters or asteroids. The project helped scientists and researchers to build an extensive database of landforms from data captured by the Mars Reconnaissance Orbiter's High Resolution Imaging Science Experiment.

The Red Balloon and the Tag challenges (both described in Chapter 3) can also be used to exemplify collective intelligence. The *Red Balloon Challenge* was completed within nine hours—a result made possible by a precise strategy from the team that won the competition: they offered mini rewards to people who sighted balloons and recruited friends to help them. The winners of the *Tag Challenge* did something similar. They won the challenge having identified three of the five suspects. In order to do so they cooperated in a team, offering monetary rewards for uploading an image of a suspect ($500), recruiting friends to help ($1 for each friend recruited), or had friends upload a picture of a suspect ($100).[52] The creators of the Tag Challenge estimate that, during the most time-critical portion of the challenge, one in three social messages were geographically targeted. The *MIT Technology Review* dubbed this ability '12 hours of separation'.

---

[50] See J. GASTIL, *By Popular Demand: Revitalizing Representative Democracy Through Deliberative Elections*, University of California Press, 2000.
[51] See P. LEVY, *Collective Intelligence: Man's Emerging World in Cyberspace*, Plenum Trade, 1997.
[52] Interestingly, another team that participated in the challenge had promised that, if victorious, they would donate the prize money to local charities.

11. Gamified publics and governance no. 3 - network theory

Networks, claims Geoff Mulgan, are the fourth infrastructure for collective intelligence (after rules, artefacts and resources). In this book, we use network theory as a (third) analytical approach to interpret the relationship between gamified governance and citizens. The essence of the principle of a network organisation is to replace multilevel hierarchies with a network of autonomous units. According to network theorists, participants of network exchange information, share resources and generate self-coordinated actions. For these reasons, networks are described as powerful tools of advocacy in domestic and supranational arenas.[53]

In her last book, Anne-Marie Slaughter distinguishes three types of networks, according to the quality and density of linkages between the individuals that populate those networks.[54] The first type is described in terms of 'cooperation'—that is, when a linked group of individuals working together carry out a prescribed task in a prescribed way. Cooperation networks can evolve into 'collaboration networks', when a linked group of individuals figure out together the best ways to carry out a prescribed task that itself may evolve. Slaughter exemplifies this typology of networks with the US military command that in 2004 was tasked with defeating al-Qaeda in Iraq.

If we translate the concepts of cooperative and collaborative networks in the framework of gamified governance we advance our understanding of the participants in these policies. The skills and competences of policy-entrepreneurs, combined with the leverage of citizens-lobbyists, are key to establishing networks of collaboration. Public challenges are a case in point. The concept of 'collaborative governance', after all, has already received attention in legal doctrine. John Donahue and Richard Zeckhauser define it as 'structured arrangements that interweave public and private capabilities on terms

---

[53] See SGUEO, *Beyond Networks*.
[54] See A.M. SLAUGHTER, *The Chessboard and the Web*, Yale University Press, 2017.

of shared discretion'.[55] Beth Noveck classifies collaborative governance as a distinctive feature of 'wiki governments'.[56] Citizen-activists seem to fit into cooperative networks. They aggregate around common concerns and values, and scatter once the cooperation is no longer needed.

There is a third type of network in Slaughter's description. This is bound to involve the former two. 'Innovation networks', as Slaughter names them, are linked groups of individuals tasked with generating new ideas, processes, and products in the service of a prescribed general goal. In this case, at different stages of the policy process, all publics described in this chapter can be engaged.

---

[55] See J.D. DONAHUE & R.J. ZECKHAUSER, *Collaborative Governance: Private Roles for Public Goals in Turbulent Times*, Princeton University Press, 2011.
[56] See B.S. NOVECK, *Wiki Government: How Technology Can Make Government Better, Democracy Stronger, and Citizens More Powerful*, Brookings Institution Press, 2009.

6. The Dark Side of Gamified Governance

In the previous chapter, we analysed the different types of citizens that might be engaged by gamified policies. We reviewed key concepts that can be used to explain why certain citizens engage when certain conditions occur. In this chapter, we move to analysing the most pressing issues related to gamified governance.

As with any topic that explores innovation in the exercise of public power, there is no shortage of strong views from both opponents and proponents. Two opposing views go head to head: innovation versus tradition, Athens versus Sparta. Advocates of gamified governance focus on the potential benefits that gamification offers in terms of the quality of policies, accountability of policy-making and legitimacy of public regulators. Gamification enthusiasts laud fun-designed policy-making for the smart solutions it provides to many of the pressing issues faced by public regulators. The most passionate go as far as to suggest that gamification is the future of democratic decision-making.

Sceptics consider this nonsense. Gamification's opponents warn against a number of regulatory challenges, including the organisational resistance to innovation in the public sector, the risk of bias or that of fraudulent use of citizens' feedback, and more generally the lack of sufficiently qualitative inputs from crowds engaged in gamified policies. Gamified governance, claim critical voices, is nothing more than a passing fad, set to disappear.

In this chapter, we review the problematic aspects of gamified governance. Reasons of concern are, in sequence: the risks and paradoxes of using incentives in policy-making, the drawbacks of collective intelligence, the interdependent issues of digital division, exclusion and ignorance, the linguistic challenges, and the threats to privacy.

With the risks defined, it is possible to address the questions of effectiveness and desirability of gamification with which we started this book. Taken together, the drawbacks analysed in this chapter seem to hamper the ability of gamified tools to attract civic expertise and use it to build better (and more inclusive) policies. Technology writer Clay Shirky once described the existence of a 'cognitive surplus' - a reference to the thousands of hours most people spend passively watching television instead of dedicating energy to creative pursuits.[1] Beth Noveck explained that there is also a 'civic surplus' provided by citizens who participate in civic sciences activities, like measuring water quality or contributing to online mapping.[2] If we look at gamified policies constrained by legal, social and technologically biases, we must admit that these are unfit to exploit positively the civic surplus of citizens. This is not, however, our final verdict. The desirability of gamified governance should be tested again adopting a reverse perspective: focusing on solutions, not issues. This task will be entrusted to the conclusions of this book.

1. Dangers of incentives

A first issue to examine is perception. There may be claims that gamification actually discourages participation. This is especially true when participants in gamified processes experience fallouts in accessibly to decision-making or develop the sense that the process itself is aimed at manipulating their conduct.

---

[1] See C. SHIRKY, *Here Comes Everybody*, Penguin 2009
[2] See NOVECK, *Smarter Citizens, Smarter State*, p. 4.

Gamification is expected to work as an incentive to foster good civic behaviour (as Richard Thaler reminds us). But what are the risks of incentivising citizens? Ruth Grant identifies three.[3] First are the unintended outcomes of incentive schemes. Incentives, in other words, may produce the opposite of the intended effects. One example is the so-called 'paradox of disincentives'.[4] The paradox lies in the fact that incentives (in our case the gamified elements) may be viewed as the outcome of an authoritarian exercise of power from the moment in which citizens perceive that they lack the ultimate control of their decisions.

For those who criticise nudging this is a crucial point. As we explained in Chapter 1, nudging is assumed to work best when the target is unaware of being nudged. Hence the problem: public policies that incentivise citizens to adopt certain behaviours are unethical if the citizens are not informed of the incentives. Theorists of nudge respond by saying that nudging maintains freedom of choice. That's true. On paper, citizens targeted by public nudges have plenty of options. But actually, a nudge - or, in our case, a gamified policy - will have failed if it does not let citizens choose certain options in preference to others. Hence the paradox: once citizens become aware of the incentives, they may decide to behave contrary to expectations. They might abstain from participating, for instance.

The second risk identified by Grant is the detrimental effect that incentives may have on individual motivations. This is especially true with monetary incentives—just think back to what happened in Stockholm with the *Street Camera Lottery*. Suzanne Mettler provocatively calls such type of incentives 'submerged policies'. She claims that monetary incentives have obscured the role of governments and exaggerated that of markets, and ultimately have resulted in citizens unaware of the benefits they receive.[5]

---

[3] See R.W. GRANT, *Strings Attached: Untangling the Ethics of Incentives*, Princeton University Press, 2012.
[4] See C.R. SUNSTEIN, *Why Nudge? The Politics of Libertarian Paternalism*, Yale University Press, 2014.
[5] See S. METTLER, *The Submerged State: How Invisible Government Policies Undermine American Democracy*, Chicago University Press, 2011.

The third, and probably more troubling, risk envisaged by Grant relates to the perpetuation of incentives. We know from the Deloitte digital survey of 1,200 government officials from seventy countries that 82% of them are focusing on improving the 'customer experience' as a primary objective of their organisation's digital strategy.[6] That is encouraging, but it may be counterweighted with the following critical argument: if people become accustomed to receiving incentives as a response to certain behaviours, they may no longer behave in the expected way once the incentives are removed. Moreover, lowering citizens' expectations could be perceived as a synonymous to poor government service.

2. The hollowing of the state

In previous chapter, we lauded the potential of collective intelligence. However, it too presents risks that public institutions should not neglect. In a famous article published at the turn of the century, H. Brinton Milward and Keith Provan analysed the progressive replacement of the public sector with a network of third-party providers and services. The 'hollowing of the state', as they termed it, raised the issue of the (perceived) legitimacy of the public sectors.[7] It could be argued that a legitimacy risk exists for public administrations when collective intelligence substitutes collective decision-making. Not by chance, Beth Noveck considers design the greatest challenge - in terms of marshalling convincing evidence for the adoption of new technologies, identifying and targeting the right publics and including the right motivational incentives - to crowdsourcing in the public sector.[8] Other risks to consider are those normally associated with collective intelligence, and which have been subsumed under the umbrella of 'groupthink'. The risks of groupthink challenge the

---

[6] See DELOITTE DIGITAL, *Digital Government Transformation*, Deloitte, 2015.
[7] See H.B. MILWARD & K.G. PROVAN, 'Governing the hollow state', *Journal of Public Administration Research and Theory*, 10, 359-379 (2000).
[8] See NOVECK, *Wiki Government*.

6. The Dark Side of Gamified Governance

notion that such deliberation always leads to better decisions. Indeed, groupthink may promote unthinking uniformity and dangerous self-censorship, thus failing to combine information and enlarge the range of arguments.[9] The majority of Americans, for instance, think that 33% of their population are immigrants, when in fact it is just 14%. There is widespread belief among Brazilians that the average age in their country is 56, when it's actually 31. Examples like this, as shown in the Ipsos Views report of 2015, abound.[10]

Amos Tversky and Daniel Kahneman were among the first to study cognitive biases and their consequences. In 1974 they described cognitive biases as the result of systematic errors associated with heuristic rules. Example: the 'anchoring bias', when an individual relies disproportionately on the first piece of information they encounter, rather than weighting all information they possess.[11] Forty years (and several studies) apart, we can identify three types of risk connected to groupthink. First is pluralistic ignorance: the danger that arises when each decision-maker in a group has too little information to solve a given problem, and instead of scrutinising the issue, further observes others in the hope of becoming wiser. But when everyone else does the same, everyone simply observes the lack of reaction, and therefore based on this very lack of reaction easily makes a wrong inference.[12]

The second risk is 'informational cascade'. This happens when people one by one adopt the opinions and actions of passers-by as valid examples of what to think or do. Just like pluralistic ignorance, the outcome may be rather petrifying. Whole crowds may behave in a stupid way and cause damage.

A third risk is 'polarisation'. Polarisation happens when people's

---

[9] See J.L. IRVING, *Victims of Groupthink* Houghton Mifflin, 1972; J.L. IRVING, *Groupthink: Psychological Studies of Policy Decisions and Fiascoes*, Houghton Mifflin, 1982.
[10] See IPSOS KNOWLEDGE CENTRE, *Ipsos Views: The Perils of Perception*, 2015, available at www.ipsos.com.
[11] See A. TVERSKY & D. KAHNEMAN, 'Judgement under uncertainty: Heuristics and biases', *Science*, 185, 1124-1131 (1974).
[12] See D. PRENTICE, 'Pluralistic ignorance' in R. BAUMEISTER & K.D. VOHS (eds.), *Encyclopedia of Social Psychology*, Sage, 2007.

attitudinal agreement is strengthened when further processing the available information in terms of deliberation or debate. Therefore, if a group is in agreement on a certain topic, whether political, religious, cultural or otherwise, they have a tendency to only view and consider information which endorses their already established opinions. People clustering into like-minded, homogeneous groups, is not beneficial to democratic deliberation, argues Cass Sunstein. The decrease of discussion across lines of perspective generates echo chambers, where people seek out only like-minded viewpoints.[13]

3. Digitally divided

We know that, to exploit collective participation, gamification has to be deeply rooted in technology. Technology, however, is also a source of risk for regulators experimenting with gamified governance. There are three risks that are particularly important. The first, to be shortly addressed, is digital division. The second regards digital exclusion and the third is related to 'digital ignorance'.

Let us begin with the risks of digital division. Biases in availability may limit participation only to those with appropriate technologies, while leaving those without access out in the cold - a problem that scholars describe in terms of a 'digital divide'.[14] Only a few of the many cases of gamified policies raised in this book were designed to engage both online and offline communities. Manor Labs provides an example of best practice: leader boards with the most voted proposals were published in local newspapers in order to engage locals without access to the internet. At the supranational level, the case of *Ozzy Ozone* stands out. This included the publication of printed

---

[13] See C.R. SUNSTEIN, *Republic.com*, Princeton University Press, 2009.
[14] On digital divide, see P. NORRIS, *Democratic Phoenix: Reinventing Political Activism*, Cambridge University Press, 2003; B. BARBER, 'Three scenarios for the future of technology and strong democracy', *Political Quarterly*, 113:4, 573-589 (1998); L.E. CEDERMAN & P.A. KRAUS. 'Transnational communication and the European demos' in R. LATHAM & S. SASSEN (eds.), *Digital Formations: IT and New Architectures in the Global Realm*, 1-35, Princeton University Press, 2005.

6. The Dark Side of Gamified Governance 141

comics related to the topic of the online game. In the majority of cases, however, gamified governance is a wholly online affair.

Indeed, as internet penetration improves worldwide, concerns about the digital inequalities will become less pressing. Take the case of the US. Over the sixteen years spanning the last four presidential elections, the percentage of Americans with internet access has risen from 63% to 88%. Smartphone ownership has doubled, from 35% to 77% of the population.[15] Yet, the US is not the standard in terms of internet penetration. In 2017, large parts of the population from emerging economies, and still significant parts of population of G8 countries suffer serious problems in access to the internet. Globally, about 50% of people in the world are using the internet. According to 2017 figures, internet penetration stands at 88% in North America, 80% in Europe, 69% in Oceania, 46% in Asia, and 31,2% in Africa. From 1995 to 2017 the number of internet users worldwide passed from 16 million (0,4% of the world population) to 3,885 million (51,7% of the world population).[16]

Access to the internet is rising, but it is still far from being universal. The case of India is telling. In Chapter 1, we mentioned the rapid spread of instant messaging apps such as WhatsApp and social media among Indians. Facebook estimates that it has 185 million active users in India, making the Indian community the world's largest user pool for the company's service. And yet the WB estimates there are still more than a billion Indians offline. According to the latest figures, over 30% of rural Indians are illiterate and 90% of CSOs operating in the country do not have a web presence and barely know how to operate a computer.[17]

Differences in access - warn authors like Benjamin Barber - may

---

[15] See PEW RESEARCH CENTER, 'The evolution of technology adoption and usage', 11 January 2017, www.pewresearch.org/fact-tank/2017/01/12/evolution-of-technology/ft_17-01-10_internetfactsheets.
[16] See internet usage statistics for 2017 at www.internetworldstats.com/stats.htm.
[17] For more details, see A.T. SILBERFELD, *Disrupting Democracy: Point. Click. Transform*. Bertelsmann Foundation, 2017.

reinforce existing political inequalities between social groups.[18] A recent investigation conducted by the non-profit Center for Public Integrity found that even though internet access in the US has improved in recent years, families in poor areas are almost five times less likely to have access to high-speed broadband than the most affluent American households. The study reveals that in the US families in neighbourhoods with a median household income below $34,800 - the lowest fifth of neighbourhoods nationally - are five times less likely to have access to broadband than households in areas with a median income above $80,700 - the top fifth.[19]

4. Digitally excluded

We should never forget that even when access to the internet is guaranteed, participatory rights are not a certainty. Or, to put it another way, if you live in a country where the internet comes without onerous restrictions on content, unchecked surveillance or repercussions for legitimate speech, then you are outnumbered, four to one.[20] Twenty-seven percent of all internet users live in countries where people can be arrested for having published or shared content online. In 2016, this happened in thirty-eight countries.

Take the case of Turkey. In the aftermath of the failed *coup d'etat* of July 2016, thousands of smartphone owners were arrested for downloading the encrypted communication app *ByLock* (available publicly through Apple and Google app stores) amid allegations that they could be among the organisers of the putsch. In seven of the countries where individuals were detained as a result of their online activities, they were also tortured. The human rights activist Ebtisam al-Saegh, for instance, reported sexual assault by security agents after

---

[18] See B. BARBER, *Strong Democracy: Participatory Politics for a New Age*, University of California Press, 1984.
[19] The full study is available at www.publicintegrity.org/2016/05/12/19659/rich-people-have-access-high-speed-internet-many-poor-people-still-dont.
[20] See FREEDOM HOUSE, *Freedom of the Net*, 2017, https://freedomhouse.org/report/freedom-net/freedom-net-2017.

her arrest in May 2017 for having criticised the State of Bahrain on Twitter.

You might be lucky enough to be in the quarter of internet users living in countries where full and free access to the internet is guaranteed, but you are still at risk. A recent report of the MIT Media Lab identifies a number of perils related to the internet, one being 'exclusion'.[21] There are certain groups - the LGBT community or indigenous people, for instance - that are systematically under-represented in (if not excluded by) online political and social discourses. In spite of what some may think, this is not a marginal issue. Now, considering the fact that less than 5% of the world's population currently lives in a 'full democracy'[22] - while nearly a third live under authoritarian rule - and that fundamental rights have diminished in almost two-thirds of the 113 countries surveyed for the 2018 Rule of Law Index, you can easily conclude that digital exclusion is a matter of global concern.[23]

5. Digitally ignorant

It might be your lucky day: you are in the minority of citizens guaranteed full access to the internet and not part of any social group at risk of exclusion. Unfortunately, you are not entirely safe. You are still at risk of being misinformed.

In November 2017, the cover of *The Economist* asked readers: 'Do social media threaten democracy?' - questioning the role of social media in spreading accurate information and enlighten politics. The article reported on a trend that had recently exploded - that of large amounts of misinformation about politics being distributed through social media platforms. The (mis-)information included

---

[21] See C. BARABAS, N. NARULA & E. ZUCKERMAN, *Defending Internet Freedom Through Decentralization: Back to the Future?* MIT Media Lab Report, 2017.
[22] See THE ECONOMIST INTELLIGENCE UNIT, Democracy Index 2018, https://infographics.economist.com/2018/DemocracyIndex.
[23] See WORLD JUSTICE PROJECT, Rule of Law Index 2017–2018, https://worldjusticeproject.org/our-work/wjp-rule-law-index/wjp-rule-law-index-2017–2018.

polarised and polarising opinions on political candidates that had been shown to impact public opinion significantly.

The role of social media in spreading hoaxes and false news, for example, has been recognised to be relevant in the close vote for Brexit in June 2016, as well an in the US presidential elections in November the same year. According to research conducted at the School of Management of Swansea University, during the US presidential election and the Brexit vote campaigns, for every original tweet created by a bot, there had been, on average, seven retweets made by humans. Allegations against Facebook were officially laid out in February 2018, when federal counsel Robert Mueller indicted thirteen Russian individuals and organisations. In the case of Brexit, the researchers at Swansea University claim that in the forty-eight hours before the Brexit referendum, Russian-linked accounts posted more than 45,000 tweets encouraging people to vote for Brexit.[24]

The more studies are published on this topic, the bigger the issue's dimension appears. In the digital age, speed is decisive. Online posts can be shared widely within minutes. Democratic institutions instead move too slowly to be effective in fighting trolls and online hate. A study on digital misinformation and junk news related to the 2017 UK General Election found that UK users shared significantly worse quality news and information, compared to German and French users (but better quality compared to US users).[25] The Reuters Institute found that many of the most prominent identified 'fake news' websites are far less popular than established news sites. However, the study claimed, the difference between false news sites and mainstream news sites in terms of interactions on social networks, specifically on Facebook, is less clear-cut.

---

[24] See Y. GORODNICHENKO, T. PHAM & O. TALAVERA, *Social Media, Sentiment and Public Opinions: Evidence from #Brexit and #USElection*, Working Papers 2018-01, Swansea University School of Management, 2018.

[25] See J.D. GALLACHER, M. KAMINSKA, B. KOLLANYI & P.N. HOWARD, 'Junk news and bots during the 2017 UK General Election: What are UK voters sharing over Twitter?', COMPROP Data Memo 2017, http://comprop.oii.ox.ac.uk/wp-content/uploads/sites/89/2017/06/Junk-News-and-Bots-during-the-2017-UK-General-Election.pdf.

Digitally misinformed citizens are not only harming themselves with distorted perceptions of reality and polarised opinions; they collectively impact on the erosion of trust of policy-makers. 'If trust in what politicians say is already low' - claims Rachel Botsman from the pages of *The Guardian* - it could soon be non-existent'.[26] Borrowing from studies on participation, we could argue misinformation decreases both the *depth of access* (i.e. the level of involvement of citizens) and the *range of access*, that is to say the breadth of civil society actors to participate.[27]

6. Linguistic barriers

Related to the problem of access to technologies is the issue of language proficiency. We know that the dominant language on the internet is English, but we are also aware of the fact that language skills are distributed unevenly across the world. Take the case of Europe. According to the World Economic Forum, the Netherlands is the nation with the highest English language proficiency in Europe, followed by Denmark, Sweden, Norway and Finland. Southern/central countries like Spain, France or Italy are all ranked lower. On paper, the EU recognises the equal relevance of all official languages. A visit to any official EU institution website is enough to realise that only key messages are translated into all languages. All other information is available only in the three main working languages of the EU: English, French and German.

Language barriers, we can claim, may repeat the separation between linguistically versatile citizens and those citizens who believe themselves not to be proficient enough in the English language to take part in online conversations, to participate in web polls, or to

---

[26] See R. BOTSMAN, 'Dawn of the techlash', *The Guardian*, 11 February 2018, www.theguardian.com/commentisfree/2018/feb/11/dawn-of-the-techlash.
[27] See J. TALLBERG, T. SOMMERER, T. SQUATRITO & C. JÖNSSON, *The Opening Up of International Organizations: Transnational Access in Global Governance*, Cambridge University Press, 2013.

engage in any other online-based participatory venue, including gamification. Even if one understands a foreign language in a technical sense, suggests Will Kymlicka, it does not mean that he/she feels comfortable in debating political issues in another tongue. Kymlicka points out that political communication is based on ritualistic components, and without knowledge of these elements, one may be unable to understand political debates.[28] We must conclude that, even if we assume that concurrent translation would have acceptable costs, the problem of mutual understanding will remain unsolved.

7. Policy cycle: front and back ends

A fourth risk of introducing gamification into policy processes is with its application to different stages and areas of governance. Let us begin with the former, using the five-stages model ideated by Howlett, Ramesh and Perl. The first stage, 'agenda setting', consists of identifying a problem and bringing it to the attention of the policy-makers; then comes the 'policy formulation', when available policy options are considered and solutions are crafted; the third stage consists of 'policy decision-making', when public regulators choose whether to act or remain inactive on a given policy item; fourth is 'policy implementation', when the adopted policy is put into practice; the fifth and last stage of the cycle consists of 'evaluation', whereby the implemented policies are analysed in order to determine how well they meet the objectives and, if necessary, are amended.[29]

At the outset, it is complicated and resource-intensive to design gamified policies. And even if they are successful in doing so, public regulators have no guarantee about the impact. Depending on the

---

[28] See W. KYMLICKA, 'Citizenship in an era of globalisation' in SHAPIRO & HACKER (eds.), *Democracy's Edge*.
[29] See M. HOWLETT, M. RAMESH & A. PERL, *Studying Public Policy: Policy Cycles and Policy Subsystems*, Oxford University Press, 2003.

stage of policy cycle - that is, 'front-end', including the stage of agenda-setting, problem formulation and policy formulation, or 'back-end', which involves policy implementation, enforcement and evaluation - gamified experiments may provoke different responses and preferences. Issues related with the implementation of policy tools in different stages of the policy cycle are common among regulators. A study on e-democracy in Europe published by the European Parliamentary Research Service in 2018 compared twenty-two cases of digital tools aimed at improving participation in Europe. Obviously not all cases analysed in the study can be described as gamified governance; but that is not the point. The point is that the study confirms that the successful implementation of digital tools is related with the policy phase where these tools are implemented.[30]

Block by Block provides a good example of gamified front-end policy and the related risks. As reported in Chapter 4, this Minecraft simulation used by UN-Habitat to engage local communities in designing public spaces has concluded twenty projects since 2012 and initiated fifteen more between 2017 and 2018. UN-Habitat is involved as participants familiarise themselves with the game and debate on how the redesign the public spaces where they live. Once the agreement is reached, UN-Habitat hands over to local authorities, who are responsible for implementing the decisions facilitated through the game. In cases like this, the regulator has limited control over the final outcomes. There were projects, reports UN-Habitat, that had to be terminated early, due to the lack of understanding or cooperation between UN civil servants and local authorities. One of the first *Block by Block* projects, for instance, aimed to redesign a sports field in the Kibera slum in Nairobi. By the end of the process the UN officials realised that the issue of land rights was unclear and decided to interrupt the simulation. Another project in Lima had to be restarted following a change in the local government.

---

[30] See EUROPEAN PARLIAMENT, *Prospects of e-democracy in Europe*, European Parliamentary Research Service, PE 603.213, 2018.

8. Policy areas

A similar discourse may be applied to the area of regulation interested by gamified policies. Let us move from the cases analysed in this book: there are three policy areas in which gamification has been developing rapidly. The first, and by far most important, is urban management. In 2016, a report by NYU Wagner and the Center for an Urban Future highlighted how mayors and city managers are using innovative approaches to ameliorate poverty, finance infrastructure work and protect the environment. The report profiled fifteen of the most innovative urban policies launched by cities over the previous decade.[31] Development aid is also important for experimentation with gamification, especially among supranational regulators. A third area of regulation in which gamification seems to have taken hold rapidly is market regulation. Think about the public challenges organised by domestic and supranational regulators. Most of these challenges are aimed at identifying better conditions for goods, services or processes of the market.

The fact that gamified governance has developed better or quicker in certain policy areas does not necessarily mean that it only fits those areas. It is, however, a clear sign of the difficult path towards harmonisation of rules and practices concerning governance - one of the dilemmas faced by public regulators. In the public arena of laws, regulators and rules described by Sabino Cassese, gamification is implemented as far as the demand of the publics meet the supply of the regulator. In urban management, development aid and market regulation there exist the conditions for the implementation of gamified governance. All these areas are characterised by an elevated number of interests at stake and highly criticised regulatory practices. In other areas these conditions are only temporary, or absent. Here innovative forms of governance - including gamification - can be delayed or not experimented.

---

[31] See NEW YORK UNIVERSITY, CENTER FOR AN URBAN FUTURE, *Innovation and the City*, 2016, https://wagner.nyu.edu/files/labs/Innovation_and_the_City_2016.pdf.

9. The new feudal society

The use of internet platforms for consultation - indeed, all experiments with digital tools (like with gamification), pose a threat to privacy. Bruce Schneier from the Harvard Law School has developed a fascinating theory. He proposes that the pervasiveness of the internet in our lives has created a new feudal society. We sacrifice complete control over our data and pledge allegiance to large corporations. These corporations, in turn, protect us from security threats. Not only corporations, but also governments, continues Schneier, are part of this new feudalism. The use of digital tools has increased the control of data by governments and decreased citizens' control of their privacy.

Gamification, as with any other digital tool for governance, relies extensively on user data. As levels of engagement increase, a larger amount of personal information is required to be shared with administrators. Verification processes also become important. Indeed identity verification processes or mechanisms to gather information about users are found in some form or another among cases of gamified governance. *Decide Madrid*, for instance, has a three-tiered system that determines the actions that participants can take. Users can decide not to register, and in this case, they are only allowed to browse site content. Alternatively, they can decide to become basic verified users. Verification is made through residence data and a mobile phone number. Basic users are allowed to participate in online discussions and create support proposals. The most important feature however, voting, is permitted only to those who register as completely verified users. Verification in this case is carried out in person or via email.

These kinds of multilevel verification systems are pretty standardised and can be found in the majority of cases of gamification analysed in this book. There are very few exceptions. One is *ABC Kindness*. This app was explicitly designed not to require any personal information to be shared, in order to allow use by underage persons. *Decidim* adopts a mid-way solution: any individual can put up a proposal; however, voting on proposals is restricted to residents of Barcelona. At the time of registration, individuals are requested to provide their residency details, which are checked against the municipality register. After this one-time check, no personal data is retained. Moreover, the platform allows the use of pseudonyms to let users maintain their anonymity in interactions with other users.

At the other end of the spectrum we find instances of gamification that are clearly privacy-intrusive. Readers might recall from recent years the case of *BinCam*.[32] In 2011 researchers at Newcastle University announced a pilot project aimed at monitoring individuals' food waste and recycling behaviour. The *BinCam* system used an augmented kitchen bin to monitor individuals' waste management activity. The idea was to install a mobile phone in the inside of the lid and capture an image of the contents every time the bin was used. The next stage involved the recruitment (through the Amazon's Mechanical Turk system) of people to evaluate each photo. Evaluators had to glean as much information as possible from each photograph, focusing in particular on the items that were recyclable. After the evaluation, the photos were uploaded to a Facebook application. The idea was to exploit the potential of social dynamics and game-like competition through a scoring system to rate each user, compare individuals' scores online and award the top users.

BinCam was abandoned because of ethical and privacy issues. One project that has not been abandoned, however, aims at rating the 'good behavior' of Chinese citizens. Initially proposed by a group of researchers at the Chinese Academy of Sciences in the late 1990s, the project entered into the trial phase in 2010, with the municipality of Suining selected as the test platform. All residents above 14 years old were rated for their actions. Not only personal data, but also activities performed by the residents of Suining were recorded,

---

[32] See A. THIEME, J. WEEDEN, N. KRAEMER, S. LAWSON & P. OLIVER, *BinCam: Waste Logging for Behavioral Changes*, Personal informatics & HCI: design, theory, & social implications: CHI 2011 Workshop 2011, www.personalinformatics.org/docs/chi2011/thieme.pdf. See also MOROZOV, *To Save Everything*.

stored and turned into grades. Grade A citizens would be given priority for social services, while D citizens would be denied licences, permits and access to social services. In 2014 the State Council, China's governing cabinet, approved the nationalisation of this rating system.

Conclusions: The Only Winning Move Is (Not) To Play

Delving into gamified governance is like opening Pandora's box. What we have found was both encouraging and deeply concerning. Gamified policies nurture civic engagement. Score one for gamification. But they have substantial costs in terms of accessibility and privacy—minus one for gamified policy-making. Fun-designed incentives help regulators to motivate citizens; yet sometimes deprive individuals of motivations. We are back where we started. Between choosing whether to be pleased—or terrified—about attempts to instill playfulness into the relationship between citizens and public regulators. This is made even more difficult by the fact that, while writing this book, processes are still unfolding. In such a stalemate, WOPR, the supercomputer programmed to predict possible outcomes of nuclear war in the 1983 American sci-fi movie *WarGames*, would probably suggest: 'the only winning move is not to play'.

This book, instead, takes a pragmatic approach. It recognises that gamification alone is not a 'game-changer'. Evidence examined in this book suggests that, in terms of advancing the quality and quantity of interactions among citizens and public regulators, gamification has not yet had any real impact. Whether this remains the case will only be revealed in time. The bottom line is that the use of gamification, in combination with the right policy tools and cautionary approaches, could help to achieve concrete institutional changes in contemporary democratic systems. Once we accept that gamification in governance is in flux, we can focus on solutions, rather than threats. In this concluding section, we will advance some proposals (or, alternatively, highlight valuable theoretical and empirical research efforts) aimed at solving six of the most pressing threats posed by gamified governance.

1. The puzzle of effectiveness

Let's begin with the practical aspects. Earlier, we discussed three 'publics' that could be engaged by gamified policy-making. Not mentioned was how they could provide valuable inputs to regulators. So, the question becomes: in which environment does gamification have the best chance of being effective?

To respond, this book suggests starting from the theory of 'mini-publics' developed, among others, by Robert Dahl and John Dryzek.[1] The basic rationale for the mini-public approach is that relatively small groups of citizens, usually recruited through random sampling, could deliver effective decisions and overcome the issues commonly faced by democratic decision-making. Thus, the root notion of mini-publics is that democracy requires a balance between diverging arguments in a context of mutually civic and diverse discussion. Citizens' juries, deliberative polls and consensus conferences are all exemplars of mini-publics. Dryzek envisages in mini-publics a solution to the risk of anti-democratic representation. He explains that deliberative processes involve mechanisms for driving and supporting interactions within and between governance networks. These networks, however, are often populated by society's elites. Hence the risk of anti-democratic representation that could narrow the context for deliberation. Even in the case of large-scale

---

[1] See R.A. DAHL, *Democracy and its Critics*, Yale University Press, 1989; S. DRYZEK, *Foundations and Frontiers of Deliberative Governance*, Oxford University Press, 2010.

participation, scholars note, participants are orchestrated by advocacy groups that can generate hundreds of thousands of submissions that are not informative nor reliable indicators of citizens' informed value preferences. Dryzek proposes as a solution the formation of small groups of citizens composed of the non-elite. These mini-publics would involve a more localised or task-specific forum purposed to reach consensus. As further clarified by Frank Fischer, through mini-publics citizens gain a better control of their relationship with experts, and for this reason can be understood as a mode of 'democratising' expertise.[2]

This book posits that gamified decision-making should not address a single societal environment, but rather operate on the logic of mini-publics, designing gamified participatory processes in a way that could attract diversified audiences. Policy-making, in other words, should be responsive to as wide a range of publics as possible in order to attract (and benefit from) skills (provided by citizen-entrepreneurs), social leverage (from citizen-activists) and personal/direct engagement (citizen-lobbyists).[3]

The OECD defines 'inclusive policy making' as that which: 'strives to include a diverse number of voices and views in the policy-making process, including traditional cultures'. According to the OECD, inclusive policy making offers a way for governments to improve their policy performance and to deliver concrete improvements in policy outcomes and the quality of public services.[4]

There are studies that advance useful recommendations for ameliorating participatory initiatives and making them more impactful. The CrowdLaw and People-Led Innovation projects are among those. The CrowdLaw project is run by the NYU GovLab and incorporates a section with suggestions for the thoughtful design of participatory platforms. Recommendations include the clarification

---

[2] See F. FISCHER, *Citizens, Experts, and the Environment: The Politics of Local Knowledge*, Duke University Press, 2000.
[3] See OECD, *Government at a Glance*, 2013, particularly 'Inclusive policy making' in ch. 8.
[4] See OECD, *Government at a Glance*, p. 146.

of demand of participation, optimisation of resources, better information systems and diversification of engagement opportunities tailored on diverse publics.

A number of public regulators that have experimented with gamification have begun to adapt. Take the cases of Decide Madrid and Better Reykjavik. Both initiatives are aimed at uniting opinions from all residents of the two cities, and channelling them into local policy-making. Not only do these participatory web platforms allow residents of the two cities to propose new local laws that other residents can vote to support, but they also let registered users start or contribute to debates, vote for or against motions and provide additional feedback.

The NYU GovLab is also the ideator, in partnership with the Bertelsmann Foundation, of the People-Led Innovation project. This is a methodology that city officials can use to determine how to become more empowered and effective by placing citizens and interest groups at the centre of problem-solving processes. Several of the best practices reported by the GovLab incorporate gamified elements.

2. Making smart uses of collective intelligence

Exploiting the potential of public participation implies a reliance on the potential of collective intelligence and avoiding its negative by-products. Stefaan Verhulst has drafted an agenda of solutions that could be used to tackle the challenges posed by the use of collective intelligence in governmental venues.[5] Verhulst suggests that there is substantial scope for integration, and mutual reinforcement, between collective intelligence and artificial intelligence. According to Verhulst, the agenda for fostering integration between these two

---

[5] See S. VERHULST, 'Where and when AI and CI meet: Exploring the intersection of artificial and collective intelligence towards the goal of innovating how we govern', AI & Society (2018), *available here* https://doi.org/10.1007/s00146-018-0830-z.

Conclusions

forms of intelligence move across three lines. The first is the possibility of using AI to scale up collective intelligence. As explained earlier, crowdsourcing human expertise involves a substantial degree of effort and may only attract narrow communities, excluding marginalised and disenfranchised groups. With the implementation of artificial intelligence, collective intelligence can be augmented. This is the case, for instance, of Regendus, a web platform that enables comments on policy proposals and generates insights from the comments received to inform regulatory decision-making. Another case in point is Assembl, an online platform for debate launched in 2017 by the AI Initiative at Harvard Kennedy School.[6] The platform blends artificial intelligence techniques with the collective intelligence of humans. To do so, it requires individuals to take on different roles, to fuel debates with ideas or to summarise previous discussions.

In the second line of integration identified by Verhulst the relationship between the two forms of intelligence is reversed. Collective intelligence, explains Verhulst, may 'humanise' algorithms, introducing collaborative design processes that could ensure appropriate attention to ethical concerns. An example is Moral Machine, a platform for gathering a human perspective on moral decisions made by machine intelligence, such as self-driving cars. Both types of intelligence, concludes Verhulst, may benefit from open governance philosophy. This is the third line of integration.

These studies share the belief that the right incentives provided to participants in crowdsourcing initiatives could further their engagement and motivation. The Open Government Directive issued in 2009 by the United States Office of Management and Budget, for instance, included a brief guideline for federal agencies, inviting them to consider offering different types of prizes to participants of

---

[6] The AI Initiative was created in 2015 at Harvard Kennedy School of Government to gather students, researchers, alumni, faculty and experts from Harvard and beyond, interested in understanding the consequences of the rise of Artificial Intelligence. See http://ai-initiative.org.

open challenges. The guideline did not only mention cash prizes, but also exemplar prizes and point solution prizes. A case in point is *Manor Labs*, the experiment in mass interpersonal persuasion that awarded Innobucks to citizens who chose to participate.

3. Ethics as usual

The use of automated systems, in which gamified elements are present, raises ethical issues. This brings us to the third challenge. What are the potential consequences of automated and gamified policy-making? From the outset, it is important to realise there is no single 'right' way to resolve ethical concerns that might arise in relation to gamified governance. Nor will one solution fit all problems. Rather, this is an issue where evidence is still very mixed. Researchers are still attempting to mitigate unintended bias and ethical pitfalls of automated decision-making systems. Results are encouraging.

The non-profit Center for Democracy and Technology have created an interactive tool that translates principles for fair and ethical automated decision-making into a series of questions (How to ensure fairness in treating data? What features of data should be considered? How can algorithms be tested?). The Center calls it the 'digital decision tool'. The questions posed by the digital decision tool are supposed to provoke thoughtful consideration of the subjective choices that go into building an automated decision-making system and how those choices could result in disparate outcomes and unintended harms.

4. Privacy matters

The issue of privacy is pervasive across experimental forms of governance, gamification included. Responses to this problem have been timid. One attempt involves blockchain technology. Blockchain enables a secure, trusted register to hold a record of account balances. In fact, the verification process adopted by blockchain technology utilises a verifying network with a multitude of independent verifying actors. In practice, no single entity can manipulate the blockchain on its own.

Several proposals are now actively being developed. In January 2018 Koinearth, an India-based start-up announced that they were studying ideas to combine traditional voting systems with blockchain, machine learning and mechanism design. Several months earlier Democracy Earth, a Californian non-profit organisation, presented a project called Sovereign. This is based on existing blockchain software platforms, but instead of producing units of cryptocurrency, it creates tokens called 'votes'. These units are assigned to registered users, who can vote as part of organisations (political parties, municipalities or governments) who set themselves up on the network. Unlike conventional voting systems, users of Sovereign can debate with each other before voting, and are allowed to assign more votes to a single issue. In order to protect users' anonymity (transactions on blockchain platforms are typically free to view to anyone), Sovereign proposes to partner with providers (ZCash for instance) specialised in anonymous transactions. On this matter, the Center for Strategic and International Studies (CSIS) suggests protecting the identity of users with a unique, private ID. Identities tied to IDs, according to CSIS, would require personal and stringent methods of verification to access.[7]

Early trials have been positive. Sovereign was trialled in an unofficial referendum in Colombia about a political deal with the rebel group FARC. Rather than a simple yes or no, voters were able to allocate 100 votes across the seven main planks of the proposed agreement. This proved that there was only one point in the agreement that people struggled to get behind (as we know, in the conventional vote the government's peace deal was narrowly rejected).

---

[7] See P. MEYLAN & D.F. RUNDE, 'Blockchains will change the way the world votes', *Center for Strategic & International Studies*, 26 January 2018, www.csis.org/analysis/blockchains-will-change-way-world-votes.

Moreover, *Active Citizen*, the gamified e-voting platform of Moscow, has run a pilot project to record citizens' answers as a transaction with the blockchain system. Transactions are then stored and sent to the network.

5. Embracing failure

What if gamified governance does not bring about the expected results - whatever they are? Embracing failure as an integral (and binding) part of policy experimentation is the fourth challenge to overcome. Policy labs are well aware of this and have developed solutions aimed at encouraging experimental collaboration, while limiting the risks of policy failure. One example is the New Urban Mechanics in Boston. This lab does not widely disclose the governmental entities involved in new initiatives. The idea is to make policy-makers less hesitant to engage in innovative behaviours.

Others have focused on ways to help policy-makers accept, or even benefit from, failures. The Centre for Public Impact, a non-profit foundation funded by the Boston Consulting Group, has done excellent work to classify failures in the public sector and to identify functional responses to such failures. It distinguishes between two forms of policy failure. Productive failures are those resulting from genuine experimentation, in complex environments, where it is impossible to determine likely outcomes. In contrast, unproductive failures include instances where failing resulted from error, oversight or poor judgment, and is thus avoidable. The challenge for policy-makers is to maximise the productivity of failure and avoid unproductive failures. Maximisation of productivity, suggests the Centre for Public Impact, comes from a number of features. The first is that failures need to be front-loaded, in order to maximise learning opportunities. Explicit learning phases included into policy programmes, the Centre suggests, may help to encourage this mentality.

To maximise productivity, failure must also be adapted to a continuous learning approach. Re-adaptation is key. Michael Saward, a political scientist, posits that democratic devices show their full potential not when used in isolation, but when used in sequence (or combination) with each other. He calls this process of re-adaptation 'sequenced innovations'. Empirical studies seem to confirm the validity of Saward's intuition. One is the report published in 2018 by the Danish governmental agency tasked with the role to foster creativity in the Danish public sector. The study (the first world's nationwide survey on government innovation) tells us that 73% of public sector innovations in Denmark are inspired (or copied) from others' solutions.

The same holds true for gamified governance. *Decidim* is a case in point. A section of the platform hosts Metadecidim, where citizens can contribute to improving the portal for future initiatives in participatory decision-making. In so doing, *Decidim* is basically trying to self-generate. More broadly, the sharing of the free software-based technology, procedures and protocols used to gamify policies among different regulators may also be considered as re-adaptation. A third and final feature suggested by the Centre for Public Impact to maximise the potential of policy failures is that failing should be small—that is, failures should be experimented with smaller programmes, in order to decrease costs. The non-profit Nesta names this last feature 'beta' and describes it as a powerful idea to apply to public policy-making. Beta approaches to policy-making helps to transform failures and complaints into opportunities.[8]

---

[8] See J. CHRISTIANSEN & L. BUNT, *Innovation in Policy: Allowing for Creativity, Social Complexity and Uncertainty in Public Governance*, Nesta, 2012.